IMMERSION
Bible Studies

JOHN

Praise for IMMERSION

"IMMERSION BIBLE STUDIES is a powerful tool in helping readers to hear God speak through Scripture and to experience a deeper faith as a result."
Adam Hamilton, author of *24 Hours That Changed the World*

"This unique Bible study makes Scripture come alive for students. Through the study, students are invited to move beyond the head into the heart of faith."
Bishop Joseph W. Walker, author of *Love and Intimacy*

"This beautiful series helps readers become fluent in the words and thoughts of God, for purposes of illumination, strength building, and developing a closer walk with the One who loves us so."
Laurie Beth Jones, author of *Jesus, CEO* and *The Path*

"I highly commend to you IMMERSION BIBLE STUDIES, which tells us what the Bible teaches and how to apply it personally."
John Ed Mathison, author of *Treasures of the Transformed Life*

"The IMMERSION BIBLE STUDIES series is no less than a game changer. It ignites the purpose and power of Scripture by showing us how to do more than just know God or love God; it gives us the tools to love like God as well."
Shane Stanford, author of *You Can't Do Everything . . . So Do Something*

IMMERSION
Bible Studies

Carol J. Miller

Abingdon Press

Nashville

John
Immersion Bible Studies
by Carol J. Miller

Copyright © 2011 by Abingdon Press

Library of Congress Cataloging-in-Publication Data

Miller, Carol (Carol J.)
   John / Carol Miller.
      p. cm. — (Immersion Bible study)
   Includes bibliographical references and index.
      ISBN 978-1-4267-0984-5 (curriculum—printed/text plus-cover, adhesive - perfect binding : alk. paper) 1. Bible. N.T. John—Commentaries. I. Title.
   BS2615.53.M55 2010
   226.5'07—dc22

                              2010042478

Editor: Jack A. Keller, Jr.
Leader Guide Writer: Martha Bettis Gee

11 12 13 14 15 16 17 18 19 20—10 9 8 7 6 5 4 3 2 1

Manufactured in the United States of America

Contents

REVIEW TEAM

IMMERSION BIBLE STUDIES

A fresh new look at the Bible, from beginning to end,
and what it means in your life.

Welcome to IMMERSION!

We've asked some of the leading Bible scholars, teachers, and pastors to help us with a new kind of Bible study. IMMERSION remains true to Scripture but always asks, "Where are you in your life? What do you struggle with? What makes you rejoice?" Then it helps you read the Scriptures to discover their deep, abiding truths. IMMERSION is about God and God's Word, and it is also about you—not just your thoughts, but your feelings and your faith.

In each study you will prayerfully read the Scripture and reflect on it. Then you will engage it in three ways:

Claim Your Story
    Through stories and questions, think about your life, with its struggles and joys.

Enter the Bible Story
    Explore Scripture and consider what God is saying to you.

Live the Story
    Reflect on what you have discovered, and put it into practice in your life.

IMMERSION makes use of an exciting new translation of Scripture, the Common English Bible (CEB). The CEB and IMMERSION BIBLE STUDIES will offer adults:

- the emotional expectation to find the love of God
- the rational expectation to find the knowledge of God
- reliable, genuine, and credible power to transform lives
- clarity of language

Whether you are using the Common English Bible or another translation, IMMERSION BIBLE STUDIES will offer a refreshing plunge into God's Word, your life, and your life with God.

1.

The Mystery of God

John 1:1–2:11

Claim Your Story

I am what you might call "directionally challenged." I can and do get lost anywhere, which makes me more than grateful for my GPS! I once got lost in my own kitchen. No, really! I had come into the kitchen for something in the middle of the night; and as I prepared to leave the kitchen, I turned off the light—the only light on in the whole house. I missed the door out of the kitchen, turned around, and became disoriented. I couldn't find a door or the light switch. I stood in the middle of the kitchen for a second and thought, *I don't believe it! I'm lost in my own kitchen!* I hasten to add that this was only for a second or two. As soon as I found and switched on the light, all was clear, obvious. The light made all the difference.

Almost everyone will admit to feeling lost in the dark at some point in their lives. It might have been in the terrors of a pitch-black cave or on a dark, unfamiliar road on a moonless night. Beyond being lost in physical darkness, human beings struggle with feeling lost in life, unsure of the next step, unclear about who they are and what they are here for, unable to find a light that would give them the knowledge they need to see the way ahead. What is the "right" direction? Is there a right direction?

Enter the Bible Story

Many times our feelings of being lost and in the dark stem from our inability to understand God. We feel like the writer of Psalm 8 as he looks at the vast number of stars and wonders about the mystery of their Creator. The God of black holes in space and the intricacies of the created order is not like us! How can we know such a God? How can we know what such a God wants of us? Someone has described our ability to understand who God is as being similar to an anteater's ability to understand quantum mechanics. We simply don't have the mind to comprehend the scope of the created order, much less eternity. How then can we know the God who authored them? How can we find our way out of such a profound darkness?

When we go to a party with people we may not have met before, it is important to engage in small talk. In order to know someone or be known by them, we have to speak. When we are honest in our speech, we reveal something of who we are. We can't know a person who will not speak to us. We are left in the dark! John speaks about the "Word" (*logos* in the Greek) being with God and in fact being God (1:1). God is speaking to us—God is revealing God's self to us. What God has always been is now being offered to us so that we can know who God is and how God relates to us. God's speech reveals God's nature, just as our true speech reveals our nature.

God does not use the kind of speech we think of when we think of one human talking with another. God's Word, in order to be understood by us mortals, becomes human: a form we can understand, a form with which we can interact. John writes, "The Word [the self-expression of God] became flesh and made his home among us" (literally, "pitched his tent"; 1:14a).

Three Questions

The overarching topic of the Gospel According to John is the nature and mission of Jesus Christ as the one who makes God known. Here is a Gospel that does not look or sound much like the other three Gospels (the Synoptics). Here we will find no parables. John sets out to answer three questions: Who is Jesus? Where did he come from? Where is he going? These questions will be answered time and time again throughout this Gospel. For example, in Chapter 9, which is the story of Jesus healing the man born blind, Jesus' opponents show *their* blindness when they

Across the Testaments

"In the Beginning"

It is no coincidence that the Book of Genesis (NRSV) and the Gospel of John begin with the same words: "In the beginning." John is making it very clear that the same God who spoke creation into existence is the God who spoke "the Word" and thus revealed God's self in Jesus. Genesis 1 was written to make clear that there is one God and only one God. That one God created everything that has been created. That God called the creation "good" (1:31). It is that God who reveals God's self by becoming incarnate ("enfleshed") in the man Jesus. In Genesis 1 God speaks—God expresses God's self—and creation appears. The self-expression of God creates reality. In John's Gospel, God expresses God's self and there is a new creation: "The Word became flesh."

say about Jesus, "We don't know where this man is from" (9:29b). The formerly blind man, however, shows his insight when he responds, "If this man wasn't from God, he couldn't do this" (9:33). Throughout this Gospel, Jesus and the Gospel writer will tell people exactly who Jesus is, where he came from, and where he is going: "Jesus . . . knew that he had come from God and was returning to God" (13:3b). Look for these statements throughout the book.

We can only speak of God in metaphor. No words of ours are adequate to contain the nature of God. Throughout the Old and New Testaments, metaphors are used for God: the rock, the fortress, the mother hen, the Father, the shepherd. John uses more than one metaphor to describe the nature of God that has been enfleshed.

In John 1:4-5 he uses the term *light* to describe what this expressed Word of God does for us. John tells us that the incarnate Word of God is "the light for all people" (1:4b). God has not sent the Word into the world for only one or two groups of people. All people are offered light. The word *world* in John is a technical term. It refers to those outside of the covenant faith community. God sent Christ for the "world," not just for those who were already religious. In John 8:12 Jesus proclaims, "I am the light of the world." The confusion concerning our place in the world, our reason for being, is cleared up when the light of the world is revealed. Our direction becomes obvious. The psalmist spoke of God's law as being "a lamp before my feet and a light for my journey" (Psalm 119:105). It shows us the way to go, the way to life, the way to God. So too the incarnate Word of God.

John also refers to the Word as life: "What came into being through the Word was life" (1:3b-4a). In this Gospel, Jesus, instead of referring to "the kingdom of God" or "the kingdom of heaven," speaks of "eternal life." All these terms mean the same thing—being present to God in a loving, trusting relationship that time cannot destroy. John describes this as being truly alive. In John, Jesus himself is referred to as life—"I am the resurrection and the life" (11:25b)—and the bearer of real life: "I came so that they could have life—indeed, so that they could live life to the fullest" (10:10). Jesus will use metaphors to describe himself in "I am" sayings scattered throughout the Gospel (e.g., 10:7). "Who Jesus is" is an overarching theme of the Gospel of John. He is the incarnation of the Word of God; he is the light that shows us the path; he is life—robust, authentic life in this world and the world to come.

The Prologue to the Gospel (the first eighteen verses) mentions most of the central themes of John's Gospel: the incarnation of the very nature of God, the testimony of John the Baptist, being born of God, the acceptance by God of anyone who receives God's Son, the glory of the Son, grace, and truth. There is a great deal of theology (study of God) in these eighteen verses! I once had a professor who studied in Switzerland under Karl Barth, a great twentieth-century theologian. Barth and his students were studying the Gospel of John. For the first two-hour class, Dr. Barth lectured on the phrase "In the beginning was the Word." Following that class, my professor was called back to the United States for a family emergency. He says that six weeks later, he returned to class. Walking in a little late, the first words he heard Dr. Barth say were, "and the Word was with God." Barth had lectured for five weeks on the first six words of the Prologue! John's Gospel is rich. The symbol for John the Evangelist is the eagle because his writing soars! Do not be fooled by John's simple vocabulary. His words have deep meaning; they are meant to be mulled over and looked at from many angles.

John the Baptist

Next to Jesus and Paul, John the Baptist is the most mentioned person in the New Testament. John was a prophet at a time when no prophet had spoken for almost 200 years. John denies that he is Elijah, the Old Testament prophet Jews believed would come preparing the way for Messiah. He also denies being the Messiah or "the prophet" (1:20-21). In John's Gospel, John the Baptist assumes a low profile. There were still followers—disciples—of John after the coming of Jesus. Our author wants to make it crystal clear that John is not on a par with the Christ. He is "the voice crying out in the wilderness" (1:23a). In fact, in this Gospel, Jesus' first disciples are former disciples of John. It is appropriate that they leave John and follow Jesus. John himself points Jesus out to them and proclaims, "Look! The Lamb of God who takes away the sin of the world!" (1:29). The Lamb of God would be a sacrificial lamb, given for sin. John testifies to seeing the Holy Spirit descend on Jesus (1:32). In the Synoptics, we see the Holy Spirit descend "like a dove" during Jesus' baptism (e.g., Matthew 3:16). The baptism of Jesus by John is not recounted in this Gospel, probably in order not to show John in a superior position over Jesus. The Holy Spirit is God. The term "Holy Spirit" is shorthand for "God present with us now." We affirm the Trinity as the three ways God reveals God's self to us: as Father or Creator; as Son—the Word who was incarnate in Jesus—and as the Holy Spirit—God with us, enabling us to be, in Paul's words, the body of Christ (e.g., 1 Corinthians 12).

One of Jesus' first followers is Andrew. Andrew's claim to fame is that whenever we see him, he is bringing someone to Jesus. Here he brings his brother, Simon Peter (1:41-42). We don't hear Andrew preach or teach, but we see him doing the most important thing one human being can do for another: He opens the door to God for the other to step through! Jesus calls disciples as well. He calls Philip (1:43). Then Philip finds Nathanael (1:45), who doesn't have much use for people from backwater places such as Nazareth.

A Voice Crying Out

"A voice crying out in the wilderness" is a quotation from Isaiah 40:3 (NRSV). In verses 1-2 the exiled house of Judah is comforted. The people will be freed from Babylon and will return to their own land. The voice that cries out informs the people that God will now return to God's people. Everyone, therefore, must make ready to receive the presence of God in their lives.

John the Baptist says he is making that announcement anew. In Jesus, God is coming to dwell with God's people. Everyone must prepare for God in Jesus Christ to "tabernacle" with God's people (another translation of "made his home" in John 1:14). As is typical in John's Gospel, John the Baptist's role is underplayed. He is not Messiah or Elijah (but see Matthew 11:14) or the prophet. He is merely the unnamed voice from Isaiah that calls the people to prepare for the coming of God. Again, Jesus Christ is tied to the Old Testament. He is the ultimate fulfillment of all the promises of God.

John the Baptist has testified that Jesus is Son of God (1:34). Does he mean "a chip off the old block" or "just like his dad"? The term "Son of God" is a metaphor. Jesus is God's "spitting image." The Son is intimately related to the Father. Today we might say he has the same DNA to indicate the closeness of the relationship. That too would be metaphor. Nathanael calls Jesus "Son of God" after Jesus tells Nathanael that he saw him "under the fig tree" (1:48-49), which obviously meant more to Nathanael than it does to us!

The Father-Son relationship in John is strong. Jesus consistently refers to God as "Father." He sees his mission as "making his father known" (17:26). In 14:8 Philip says to Jesus, "Lord, show us the Father." Jesus responds, "Whoever has seen me has seen the Father" (14:9b).

It seems strange, then, that people are continually ascribing to God the Father things they would never in a million years ascribe to Jesus. For example, how many well-meaning but utterly thoughtless people have said that some young person's death is "the will of God" or "all part of the plan"? Yet no one would ever associate Jesus' will with the death of the innocent. We need to remember what John emphasizes—that Jesus reveals

God. Jesus shows us the nature of God. This is at least part of what it means to say that Jesus is the Son of God. Our theology, our thinking about God, must be consistent; and it must be coherent. We cannot believe contradictory things. Either Jesus reveals God or he doesn't. Good theology makes sense.

The First "Sign"

The final text in this session, 2:1-11, describes the first of the signs that Jesus performs, turning water to wine. John calls them "signs," not "miracles." These unique actions of Jesus are signs of God's presence in Jesus, and they are signs of God's desired relationship with us. Here Jesus shows the abundance and richness of life with God. In Jesus' parables in the Synoptic Gospels, a banquet or party is a symbol for the kingdom of God (e.g., Luke 15:11-32). Even though those parables are not found in John, I don't think we are too far off if we say that in this sign Jesus is showing us the abundance that is life with God. The point of signs is not that Jesus does what is not possible for people to do. Neither signs in John nor miracles in the Synoptics are magic tricks. They are not proofs. The point of the signs is to show the nature of the relationship God chooses to have with humanity. Jesus' signs in John have to do with abundance, life, sight, and self-giving love. The point is not to be "wowed" that Jesus turned water into wine. The point is to see that God is bringing life and sight and acceptance to all people.

The queen in *Alice in Wonderland* said that she was quite capable of believing "six impossible things before breakfast." Many people today seem to think that faith means just to believe that Jesus did strange signs or miracles—that we must simply set reason aside and believe. But that is not faith; believing "six impossible things" does not draw us closer to God. The signs show us what God is bringing to God's people. We are not called to see the signs that Jesus does as "proofs" that he is the Son of God. Rather, the signs show us specifically the nature of God—who God is and what God wants for us. It is that good news in which Jesus calls us to put our trust.

Live the Story

The Gospel of John soars with theology that attempts to touch the mystery of the God who is beyond us yet incarnates his nature in Jesus of Nazareth. At once we are asked to contemplate the transcendent God and the God with us. Perhaps one way to make John's words our own is to think about one small part of the text for a day or two—sort of like Professor Barth! Who is God? How does God want to relate to you? Think of Jesus as the incarnate Word. Then remember what you can of Jesus' words and actions in all the Gospels. What is God saying to you through Jesus?

To see the God of all creation as presented in the words and life of Jesus can really turn on the light. What does this God want from us? What is this God calling us to? Here is a way we can see and follow. Here is a way out of the dark and into the light of God.

2.

Jesus Offers Life

John 2:12-22; 3:1-21; 4:4-42; 6:1-59

Claim Your Story

In Arthur Miller's play *The Price*, a middle-aged couple looks back at their life so far. Although they had planned out their lives, gotten their degrees, and had their goals in order, nothing much had happened. The wife says to her husband, "Everything was always temporary with us. It's like we never were anything, we were always about-to-be."[1] Perhaps that sentence sums up the dissatisfaction of many people today. For all our trying, restlessness remains. Life lacks a center. More than a few people come to the last quarter of their lives; look over their shoulders toward the past; and think, "Is that all there is?"

The restlessness is like a hole in our lives. We feel as though something is missing. There needs to be more. In our "thing"-filled society we often think it is just a lack of things that makes us restless. Those of us who are middle-class have a long history of trying to fill that hole in our lives with stuff—new stuff, shiny stuff, the latest stuff, expensive stuff, the "in" stuff. My favorite bumper sticker is "The one with the most toys when he dies, wins." It points up the absurdity of trying to find a life worth living in the accumulation of things.

Perhaps others think that their restlessness stems from a lack of adventure or a lack of attention. Whatever you think the cause is, you may long for something just out of reach.

"Thou hast formed us in Thine own Image, and our hearts are restless till they find rest in Thee." Thus wrote Augustine after his conversion.[2]

When have you known this restlessness? Does Augustine's statement resonate with your experience?

Enter the Bible Story

In the texts from John, Jesus is offering an answer to that haunting
question: "Is that all there is?" His answer is, "No! That is not all there is!"
There is a new life, and it is available to everyone! In 2:12-22, Jesus brings
to a screeching halt business as usual in the Temple at Jerusalem. The
Temple was the heart of Judaism and the heart of the nation of Israel. It
was symbolically the residence of God. The chief priests were in charge of
the Temple. It was they who must have allowed the dealers to set up shop
in its precincts. It was they who had authority over what went on there.
Jesus entered the Temple and cleansed it from exclusiveness, moneygrub-
bing, and hunger for power. The authorities demanded to know what right
he had to challenge what went on in the Temple. The answer was shocking. Jesus pointed to his own coming death and resurrection as his authority (2:19). He himself incorporates the holiness that had always been
associated with the Temple. Jesus, not the Jerusalem temple, had become
the sign of God's new life. This life is offered to everyone through Christ's
sacrifice and through his power to create life. The temple that matters is
not a building but Christ himself. He is the one in whom God's acceptance
and love are centered.

Isaiah had seen a future temple in which all peoples will experience
"joy in my house of prayer" (56:7, NRSV). This temple "will be called
a house of prayer for all nations" (56:7b, NRSV). The Temple that Jesus
entered was not even close to becoming what Isaiah prophesied. Jesus,
therefore, "cleanses" it. Jesus Christ becomes the true Temple. This same
idea is found also in Revelation: "I didn't see a temple in the city, because
its temple is the Lord God Almighty and the Lamb" (21:22). Something
richer, fuller, more "real" has come in Jesus. It is a fulfillment of the true
Temple. In Christ, God has brought real life. No one is excluded. The
door to God is open to all people. Here is Isaiah's prophesied temple,
the center of acceptance and joy.

Nicodemus

In 3:1 we meet Nicodemus, a Jewish leader who sees in Jesus the Temple-cleanser "a teacher who has come from God." Nicodemus comes to Jesus because he has seen signs and because, perhaps, he hopes that Jesus can help quiet the restlessness in his own soul. He comes at night, looking for the light. He trusted in the signs he had seen, but belief in signs was not enough. Sign-faith does not go to the heart. A person may come to the front door of a house; but in order to have a relationship with the one inside the house, more is required: One must open the door and go in. Believing a set of things about God is not the same as believing in God. Nicodemus' "believing" in Jesus had to be more than faith in the signs he had seen. Jesus tells him, "You must be born from above" (3:3). Jesus has come from "above." If a person wants to know Jesus and what he offers, that person must be born in a new way—no longer focused on the earthly, but focused on God. In Paul's words, "So then, if anyone is in Christ, that person is part of the new creation" (2 Corinthians 5:17a).

His earthly focus is why Nicodemus continually misunderstands Jesus—to the outrageous point of wondering how one could reenter his mother's womb! Nicodemus was centered on the earthly, but Jesus is the man from heaven. If Nicodemus truly had ears to hear, he would comprehend what Jesus says: "You are a teacher of Israel and you don't know these things?" (3:10). We will see throughout this Gospel that people continually misunderstand Jesus because they are thinking literally, while Jesus is thinking spiritually. They do not see who Jesus is. They do not believe.

Eternal Life

In 3:5 Jesus speaks of "the kingdom of God." This is a rare use of the term in John. In the Synoptic Gospels it is the usual term that Jesus uses. It has more the flavor of kingship than place. To be in the Kingdom is to be living under the reign of God: God's will is central; knowing God is Kingdom living. Most often in John's Gospel, Jesus speaks instead of "eternal life" (see 3:15). Like the kingdom of God, eternal life is that living relationship with God that begins now and cannot be destroyed by death. It is the product of putting one's trust in Christ. The word *believe*

Being "Lifted Up"

Jesus speaks too of being "lifted up" (3:14) in a reference to the Old Testament story in which Moses fashioned a bronze snake and had it raised up so that those who saw it might be healed. So Christ will be "lifted up" on the cross (see 12:32-33) that all might see the true nature of God in him, and seeing, might turn to him in trust.

Jesus is alluding to an odd story in Numbers 21:4-9 in which the people of Israel complain bitterly against God and Moses. God then sends poisonous snakes among them, and several die. God tells Moses to make a bronze serpent and to lift it up on a pole. Anyone who looks to the serpent will be healed. Those who look to the cross and see God's self-giving love there will be healed from sin, just as the Israelites were healed from snakebite.

is a key word in John. It does not mean giving assent to an idea so much as trusting in the same way we trust someone who is close to us—someone we would trust with our life. To believe is, in John, an action. If we trust what Christ is showing us, if we trust who Christ is for us, then we will act, we will follow. We enter into eternal life by trusting: "Everyone who believes in him . . . will have eternal life" (3:16).

This invitation to a living relationship with God is offered to the religious, like Nicodemus, and to the "irreligious" (we are about to meet her). All that is required is to open the door and walk in—to trust God enough to take that first step. In 3:16 John writes that "God so loved the world that he gave his only Son, so that everyone who believes . . . will have eternal life." The word *world*, remember, means those who have not turned to God. These are the ones God loves and yearns for—like Luke's loving father in the parable, gazing down the road to catch a glimpse of the prodigal. The relationship with God that Augustine thirsted for is offered in Christ to everyone.

The Samaritan Woman

The Samaritan woman at the well is the poster child for "the world." She was a Samaritan—a people generally detested by good, religious Jews;

she was a woman, which made her second-class; and she was counted as promiscuous, which put her outside of the community. She came to the well at noon, the hottest part of the day, to draw water because she knew that no other women would be there. She didn't want to be snubbed. It might be good to remember that women in Samaritan and Jewish society were not allowed to divorce their husbands. She had been the one who, more than once, had been tossed aside. Now she was living with a man. She was vilified, but she was also a victim.

Jesus asks her for a drink. She is suspicious—why is he condescending to speak to her? He offers her water—offers it for the asking: "If you recognized . . . you would be asking . . . he would give" (4:10). No question about it. If she could see the nature of God in him, she would ask and he would give. But, like Nicodemus, she heard on a literal plane. John uses irony here as she asks, perhaps in a mocking tone, "You aren't greater than our father Jacob, are you?" (4:12). If you can answer the question "Who is Jesus?" you will know the answers to the other two questions. And you will take what he offers. There is no, "If you straighten up and earn it, I'll give you living water." There is simply, "If you recognized . . . you would be asking . . . he would give." And the thirst of the soul would be satisfied.

She attempts to turn the topic of the conversation away from her marital history by getting him to talk about religion (4:19-20). The Samaritans had built a temple on Mount Gerizim. The Jews and Samaritans hated each other and each other's temples. So the woman thought she could get a pretty good debate going here. But no luck. There will be worship neither on Gerizim nor in Jerusalem, says Jesus (4:21). (Remember that at the time of John's writing, the Temple in Jerusalem no longer existed.) Worship, says Jesus, must be worship in the spirit. People should not be worrying about the place. It's not about the earthly; it's about the heavenly.

The woman, impressed by Jesus' knowledge of her, alerted the other villagers that she had found Messiah. After spending two days with him, the villagers moved past sign-faith into a living faith based on knowing him. Jesus saw these people, the woman and the villagers, entering "eternal life" (4:36b). Pharisees and Samaritans, the religiously pure and the impure, men and women, all are welcome to know God and to live in the life that God gives. This is grace: to be invited to life with God.

The last text for this session is especially long. It begins with the feeding of the 5,000, the only miracle story found in all four Gospels (6:1-15). Andrew shows up again, bringing someone to Jesus—the little boy with the loaves and fish. If we would only bring Christ what we have with honest hearts, he would do the rest. Maybe our loaves and fish are the one shred of trust we have. Andrew was embarrassed; but still he came, trusting Jesus to do something with what he had to offer. The crowds saw the sign of the feeding of them all. This sign is followed by the strange story of Jesus walking on the water (6:16-24). Throughout the Bible, water—especially the sea—is a symbol of chaos. In Genesis 1 God brings order out of "the deep." Jesus also stills the storm on the sea (Mark 4:35-41). In Revelation a new heaven and new earth replace the former heaven and earth, and "the sea was no more" (21:1). The one who spoke creation out of chaos walks on the sea.

Believing in Jesus, Believing in God

The next day, the crowds catch up with Jesus; but he is not impressed with their kind of "following." These people don't even have sign-faith: "I assure you that you are looking for me not because you saw miraculous signs but because you ate all the food you wanted" (6:26). The conversation turns to the nature of doing "what God requires" (6:28). Jesus answers, "This is what God requires, that you believe in him whom God sent" (6:29). Believing—putting our active trust in the God we see revealed in Jesus—is what God requires. If a person believes in God, that person will be living in God's love and doing God's will. There is no other definition offered in John of doing what God requires. It is the same in all the Gospels: "Why do you call me 'Lord, Lord' and don't do what I say?" (Luke 6:46).

Amazingly, the crowd (who just saw him feed the 5,000) demands a sign! They want something like manna: bread from above that they could have every day. Jesus answers with one of the "I am" sayings, which we will look at more closely in a future session. He declares himself to be "the bread of life" (6:35). Jesus is all about life: eternal life, life-giving water, abundant life, the food (bread) that ensures life. "What came into being through the Word was life" (1:3b-4a).

Jesus also speaks about his relationship to God the Father, which he does often in the Fourth Gospel. What he has, he has from God. He has not come to do his own will but God's will. He is obedient to the Father. John 6:40 is a restatement of 3:16: "This is my Father's will: that all who see the Son and believe in him will have eternal life, and I will raise them up at the last day."

Although in John's account Jesus made no reference to the bread and wine as his body and blood as he shared the last meal with his disciples before his arrest and crucifixion (see Chapter 13), we will find that language here in Chapter 6. Jesus begins by declaring that "whoever believes has eternal life" (6:47). To trust the God being made visible in Christ is to enter, here and now, into eternal life, life lived with God. Jesus declares himself to be the living bread that came from God. This bread destroys the power of death. This bread is Christ's flesh—his sacrificial love.

This "bread" language sparks a huge debate among the crowd. Once again, Jesus was being taken literally when he was speaking spiritually. If they had recognized God in him, they would have known how to interpret his words. Jesus attempts to make it clear in 6:63: "The Spirit is the one who gives life and the flesh doesn't help at all. The words I have spoken to you are spirit and life."

Again and again and again, Jesus offers all comers life in relationship with God: that birth from above, that living water, that bread of which one may eat and not die (6:50). The offer is made to all people who will put their trust in what they see in Jesus. This is the offer of satisfaction for the hungry soul. No one is turned away: "If you recognized . . . you would be asking . . . and he would give."

Live the Story

What is life—the kind of life that makes you feel that you are where you belong, doing what you should be doing? When have you felt closest to God? When have you felt fulfilled? My guess is that it wasn't when you were buying some electronic goodie that was this year's must-have. Can you identify a time in your past that you could affirm as "really living"? Have you been trying to fill that need for God with something else? It may be a good thing; it may be learning or art or a thousand things that are good in themselves. But only God can be God.

Many, many people have trouble trusting God with their lives. They hold on tightly to the way they do things and to what they value. But when we insist on being the object of trust, we make a very small package—not nearly enough to fill the God-shaped hole! And we are lonely, for we are made to be in relationship with our God. C. S. Lewis said that when he was an atheist, he did not believe in God and was mad at God for not existing![3] We need God, and no substitutes will do. Remember, in the Gospels, to trust is to act. Can you take one step in obedience? Can you relinquish your hold on one thing? Jesus, in John's Gospel, again and again invites any and all to drink deeply of life. He offers it to saint and sinner alike. God offers us real living not because we are good, but because he is good. He is the living water, the bread of life.

---

[1] From *The Price: A Play* (Penguin, 1985); page 18.
[2] From *Confessions*, Book I.
[3] From *Surprised by Joy: The Shape of My Early Life*, by C.S. Lewis (Harcourt, Brace and Company, 1955); page 115.

3.

Do You Want to Live?

John 5:1-18, 19-47; 9:1-12, 13-41

Claim Your Story

What do you really want? I've known people to say that they want all sorts of things, but their actions don't show it. This seems to be the case especially when some people complain. One estimate I read somewhere said that more than sixty percent of those who complain, complain to someone who can't fix the problem. You have to wonder if they want the problem solved or if they just want the right to complain about how they were wronged!

Maybe you've heard people in a congregation say they want to grow, but the things they do don't support that stated desire. They don't want too many new people because they might have different ideas from those in "power." The congregation doesn't bother to learn hospitality; they don't invite people to worship or to church activities—in fact, they seem to work against the very thing they say they want! They secretly like the church the way it is; they don't want anything to change, forgetting that everything changes and nothing stays the same. If you're not growing, you're shrinking! The only things that don't change are things that are not alive.

We've all known people who complain about their jobs but then don't get the training to do something else. "Better the devil you know than the devil you don't know" seems to be their motto. How often have you seen people settle for the familiar, where they know their role and what's coming next, rather than break out of the box to try something new? When have you done it yourself? When have you made excuses for not growing, for postponing needed change? Where have you chosen just not to see?

Enter the Bible Story

Healing a Man Who Was Sick

Thirty-eight years to make it a few yards? Thirty-eight years? Is it surprising that Jesus in John 5:6b asked the man, "Do you want to get well?" You really have to wonder if the man did want to get well or if he had become content with lying by the pool. He actually made excuses! "When I'm trying to get to [the pool], someone else has gotten in ahead of me" (5:7). I wonder if the man wanted to say "no" in response to Jesus' question. But how could he? How could he say that he had chosen not to live? He picked up his mat (thereby breaking the commandment about not working on the sabbath). Now that he could walk, he had to find somewhere to go and someone to be! He did not know who healed him, which seems a shocking lack of curiosity on his part (5:13). The upside was that he couldn't "rat out" Jesus to his opponents when they confronted him. Then Jesus found him later and told him not to "sin anymore in case something worse happens to you" (5:14). This was almost unheard-of for Jesus. He did not usually connect illness with sin (as we will see shortly in John 9).

This is also a text that shows the one healed in a poor light: He made excuses for thirty-eight years of failure, he didn't seem interested in who Jesus was, and then he was hunted down by Jesus so that he could be told to stop sinning. And then he used his newfound locomotion to go tell the Pharisees that it was Jesus who healed him on the sabbath, which immediately led to Jesus' persecution by his opponents! Yet he was still healed! Well, maybe I judge him too harshly; others have seen it differently. But the question—one of many evocative questions that Jesus asked—still remains: "Do you want to get well?"

John marks the healing of this man with the beginning of the persecution of Jesus by his opponents (5:16). These opponents, the local Jewish leaders, seemed unable to see Jesus as anything more than a threat to their

Jewish Pressure to Keep the Faith

In Jesus' day, community identity and solidarity were particularly important to the Jewish community. The Jewish people were once again overrun by a foreign power. It had been the Greeks before the time of Jesus; now it was the mighty Roman Empire. Roman soldiers were garrisoned in Jerusalem; and a Roman official, Pontius Pilate, served as governor of the territory.

The Romans were never able to break the Jewish people. As the pressure on them mounted, the pressure within Judaism also mounted. If you were truly a Jew, you would show yourself to be one of the group by being circumcised, keeping kosher, and observing the sabbath. Just as the Jewish exile Daniel in the Book of Daniel held to all the rituals of his faith no matter how much he was threatened, so in Jesus' day the community exerted pressure from within to "keep the faith" by the observance of these outward signs.

Jesus moves beyond simply keeping these symbols of community, which are worthless if not centered on love for God and neighbor. The Jewish leaders seemed to have no interest in the fact that a man who had been ill for thirty-eight years had been healed. In Chapter 9 they will show no joy in the giving of sight to a man born blind. Jesus in the Gospels condemns them numerous times for substituting rule-keeping for love and compassion (see Matthew 12:3-13; 23:23; Mark 7:6-13; Luke 6:9).

authority. They were religious people, constantly thinking about the requirements of their religion. But they were so wrapped up in keeping the letter of the law that they could not see the enfleshed loving-kindness of God when it was standing right in front of them. Sometimes being "religious" can be a way of avoiding God; we fool ourselves into thinking that by keeping some set of rules or rituals, we are engaging God. Sometimes folks hide in church to avoid having to deal with God.

In 5:17 Jesus declares that "my Father is still working and I am working too." The term *father* as a metaphor for God was not unheard-of in Judaism, but here Jesus' opponents took it as a blasphemous statement—that Jesus was declaring himself equal with God (5:18).

About the Scripture

"The Jews"

John has sometimes been accused of being anti-Semitic because he speaks so harshly of "the Jews." This is something of a technical term for John. Remember that Jesus was a Jew, the disciples were Jews, and most of the people in the New Testament stories are Jews. In passages in which Jesus is challenged by "the Jews" or plotted against by them, it makes the most sense to understand that John is speaking of the Jewish authorities, the leaders (for example, John 5:10 or 7:1b). It is widely held that the author of the Fourth Gospel was, at the time of writing, engaged in a dispute with the Jewish leaders of his day, which has probably colored the presentation of Jewish leaders throughout the Gospel. This terminology should never be used to attack the Jewish people.

John 5:19-47 represents one of the telltale features of John's Gospel: Jesus delivers one of a series of long monologues. Here he explains the relationship that he has with God the Father. Jesus' actions were the right actions because God had given authority to Jesus to make God visible through word and deed. In these verses Jesus and the Father are intimately linked, yet Jesus is subservient to the Father. Jesus does not act on his own initiative—"I can't do anything by myself" (5:30a); rather, he does whatever the Father does. The Father has given to Jesus authority concerning the two main functions of God: to bring life and to pass judgment (5:21-22). But in fact, in several places in John neither the Father nor Jesus needs to pass judgment. We do that ourselves by our response to the incarnation of the Word of God (see John 3:19-21).

Jesus then lists the witnesses to his authority to do the things he saw God doing: God, John the Baptist, the works that Jesus does through the Father, the Scriptures, and Moses. Thus, to ignore Christ is to ignore God at work in him. John adamantly affirms that in Jesus we see the very nature of the one God.

Healing a Blind Man

Chapter 9 is the delightfully written story of the man born blind. The disciples turn Jesus' attention to the blind man with an outrageous theological question: "Rabbi, who sinned so that he was born blind, this man or his parents?" (9:2). What kind of question is that? How could someone who was born blind have committed a sin in utero? There was an assumption on the part of many in Jesus' day (and many today) that deformities or illnesses are some kind of "punishment" for sin. In the Old Testament, the Book of Job is an argument against such thinking. Jesus rejects the disciples' assumption (9:3).

Jesus then sounds one of the themes of John's Gospel, that of light and darkness (see 1:4b-9). We know that wherever light enters a space, darkness cannot exist. The presence of Jesus has that kind of effect in the Gospels. When he is present, death turns to dust, illness turns to health, and rejection turns to acceptance. I have always kept that understanding of darkness—the absence of light—in my thinking about the nature of Jesus. In 9:4-5 Jesus utters another of the "I am" sayings: "I am the light of the world." Light allows us to see. The Light of the World allows us to see the nature of God.

The blind man receives his sight in verse 7. In verses 10-28 he is cross-examined, first by bystanders, then by the Pharisees. He tells and retells the story to the point of exasperation. Finally, in verses 28-29, the Pharisees make the key statement of the story: "You are his disciple, but we are Moses' disciples [the giver of the law]. We know that God spoke to Moses, but *we don't know where this man is from*" (italics mine). The Pharisees are right on two levels. First, the formerly blind man has become a disciple of Jesus. There is a progression in the story of the growth of his faith. When asked in verse 17 to declare who Jesus is, the man replies, "He's a prophet." In verse 25 he says, "I don't know whether he's a sinner. Here's what I do know: I was blind and now I see." In verse 33, in an attempt to instruct the Pharisees in theology, he boldly proclaims, "If this man wasn't from God, he couldn't do this." Finally, when asked by Jesus if he believes in the Son of Man, the man says, "Lord, I believe." Here is the progress of a human being from hopelessness to faith.

Second, the Pharisees angrily deny the need for any instruction on the topic of God; then they proclaim that they do not know where Jesus came from. That, at least, was the truth!

John rams home his point about light and dark, and seeing and not seeing, in verses 30-33, the long lecture to the Pharisees by the man in which he declares, in effect, that it is perfectly obvious that Jesus had come from God. John practically shouts, "Even a blind man can see!" Jesus caps off the episode by telling the Pharisees, "If you were blind, you wouldn't have any sin, but now that you say, 'We see,' your sin remains" (9:41). Their blindness was willful. They refused to see a God who did not fit in with their judgmental form of religion. They declared that they saw God when they did not. There is an old adage: "There are none so blind as those who will not see." How easy it is to filter out whatever does not fit our preconceived ideas! When have you made a poor decision by seeing, at the time, only what you wanted to see?

Jesus' authority and power to act are the indicators that Jesus has come from God. Therefore, to hear what Jesus says is to hear God's words; to see the actions Jesus performs is to see what works God wants done. Jesus is the "image of the invisible God" (Colossians 1:15). His words and works make it plain that he is God's agent, God's Son. The only intelligent thing to do in that case is to begin to follow.

About the Scripture

Jesus and God the Father

In John's Gospel the intimate connection between God the Father and Jesus is central. But it can be confusing when we try to understand the intricacies of that relationship. In John 10:30 Jesus declares, "I and the Father are one." For some, that is enough to decide that it is proper to say that "Jesus is God." However, you will not find such a statement in any passage of Scripture. The word *one* in this case is neuter in the Greek. For it to mean that Jesus and God are the same person, "one" would have to be masculine. Jesus is not speaking of equality but of being in tandem, in synch with the work of God. In John 14:28 Jesus says, "The Father is greater than me." Jesus is the physical incarnation of God's nature, God's self-expression. Jesus always points beyond himself to the Father. His "job" is to glorify the Father—that is, to make the nature of the Father known to all people.

Live the Story

Where have you chosen to be blind because what was right in front of you didn't fit in with what you wanted to see? Was it in a relationship with someone or in some political wheeling and dealing by a candidate or party you aligned yourself with? Was it some unpleasant truth about yourself that you chose not to hear? Sometimes people choose to stay away from honest conversation with others and listen mostly to themselves. In that way they can build up in their minds a little world in which they are right and the things they do and think go unchallenged. They find it inconvenient to deal with other people's perceptions or even objective realities. If you talk mainly to yourself, you'll rarely be contradicted.

Have you perhaps found your thoughts about God to be part of a little world that you have made for yourself? Have you even invented a God who—amazingly—agrees with you on almost every issue? Jesus came for many reasons. Perhaps one was to shake us out of our little worlds in which we are in control of deciding the nature of God. Do you really want to know God, or are you content to sit by the pool and complain? Do you want to see God, or have you already decided for yourself who God is? Stepping out of your "comfort zone" is scary; but that's where God is— waiting for you to pick up your mat and walk.

4.

The Law and Freedom

John 7:1–8:11, 31-38

Claim Your Story

"Just tell me what to do, and I'll do it!" Have you ever prayed that prayer? Do you sometimes think like that when you consider what God wants from you? Do you feel that a list of do's and don'ts from God would be a great help? *Just give me the list, and I'll work on doing the do's and avoiding the don'ts.* When asked the question "Are you saved?" have you ever said, "Well, I try to do what's right." If you're the kind of person who would like a checklist to live by and if you feel that the Bible must have that kind of list in there somewhere, then the Pharisees might appeal to you.

Have you been tempted to reduce your faith to the keeping of a set of rules? Some people view the Bible as if it were a series of "hints from Heloise" on how to stay on God's good side—that the Scriptures are all about you and what you need to do and how you can make yourself acceptable to God by walking the "straight and narrow." There's a desire for control in most people. If you have the right list, the right guidelines, you can set yourself up as the one who acts, the one who saves, the one who is in control. If only you can keep enough laws, you can be free.

Enter the Bible Story

How Do We Keep God's Law?

Jesus had a way of getting right to the heart of things. He said to the Jewish leaders, "Didn't Moses give you the Law? Yet none of you keep the

Law" (John 7:19). The leadership had been critical of Jesus because he had broken the Jewish law by healing the man at the pool on the sabbath (see John 5:18). In John 7:19-24, Jesus confounds his critics by pointing out that a male infant in Judaism was to be circumcised on the eighth day of life, even if that day is the sabbath. They believed that working on the sabbath in that case kept the law. Why then, he asked, was not the act of healing a man's whole body on the sabbath seen as sabbath-keeping? Jesus confronts them with the fact that their way of keeping God's law was arbitrary and wooden. Many of the Pharisees had made God's law into a list of do's and don'ts. In fact, they wrote more laws and rules to go along with them! In Mark 7:1-13 Jesus takes the Pharisees to task for all their rules and regulations, which they use to make themselves seem righteous while passing judgment on others. Compassion and love for the neighbor did not seem to enter into their decision as to whether an action was to be counted as keeping the law or breaking the law.

There is an echo here of Jesus' teaching in Mark 2:27, "The Sabbath was created for humans; humans weren't created for the Sabbath." Luke 14:3-5 (NRSV) reads:

> And Jesus asked the lawyers and Pharisees, "Is it lawful to cure people on the sabbath, or not?" But they were silent. So Jesus took him and healed him, and sent him away. Then he said to them, "If one of you has a child or an ox that has fallen into a well, will you not immediately pull it out on a sabbath day?" And they could not reply to this.

Clearly, in Jesus' mind the sabbath was truly kept only when it was built on compassion and love for the neighbor. Jesus had no interest in law-keeping for its own sake. He warned the leaders, "Don't judge according to appearances. Judge with right judgment" (John 7:24), meaning that instead of only looking at the surface appearance of his deeds, they needed to see God at work in them. The law, for which Jesus' opponents were so concerned, was truly God's law only when the nature of God was honored through it. Jesus had shown by his teaching and also by his actions that the nature of God is characterized by compassion, forgiveness, mercy, and *hesed* (loving-kindness).

So far, his detractors had ignored the healing of a man ill for thirty-eight years and the feeding of the five thousand. They will, in a short while, also ignore compassion for the woman caught in adultery, the healing of a man born blind, and the raising of the dead! None of these events moved them at all. Their law-keeping, which they used to prove their closeness to God, revealed them as far away from the nature of God.

Again and again, Jesus' argument will be that if his opponents really knew God, they would clearly see God reflected in the person and works of Jesus. The crowds at the Festival of Booths (John 7:1-44) were debating the question of Jesus' true identity. Those arguing against his being from God based their argument on the fact that they knew where Jesus had come from, by which they meant Galilee. Once again the people were thinking only on an earthly, literal level while attempting to discuss the acts of God. "Where is Jesus from?" is one of the core questions of the Gospel. If they had known the spiritual answer in addition to the geographical one—which should have been clear from Jesus' actions—there would have been no debate.

As with the woman at the well, Jesus freely offers any and all in the crowd thirst-quenching water. But he goes further this time: "Out of the believer's heart shall flow rivers of living water" (John 7:38, NRSV). The Jews used the term *heart* to refer to the inner person. It was that place from which came the deepest thoughts of an individual. To accept the water that Jesus offered was to be filled with "living water" that would become central to that person's inner self. John names that "living water" as the Holy Spirit. Those who trusted in Christ would become themselves sources of the life that the Spirit gives. This living water at once brought a person into a right and good relationship with God and began to make that person more and more Christlike. There were no preconditions for obtaining any of this. One need only ask.

The chief priests and the Pharisees were trying to have Jesus arrested, but it wasn't working out very well. The police came back empty-handed, saying, "No one has ever spoken the way he does" (7:46). The Pharisees replied that it was foolish to believe anything the crowds believed. The crowds of common people, they said, did not know the law and were

About the Scripture

Jewish Religious Festivals

John uses the major Jewish religious festivals to show Jesus as their fulfillment. The Passover, which is mentioned more than ten times, is associated with the death of Jesus (see, for example, 2:13, 23 and 12:1, 12, 20). In Chapter 10, the festival is Hanukkah. In 7:1-14, 37, the Feast of Booths or Tabernacles (also called Sukkoth) is the backdrop for Jesus' call for the crowds to come to him for relief from their thirst. On each day of the eight-day festival, there was an elaborate water ritual. The priest would bring water in a golden pitcher from the Pool of Siloam and with great ceremony pour it over the altar in the Temple. This water-libation commemorated God giving water from the rock during the Exodus (Numbers 20). Jesus stood up on the last day of this festival to invite all who thirst to come to him. If they do, "rivers of living water" will flow, not from the rock, but "from within."

"under God's curse" (7:49). These particular Pharisees revealed their lack of love for the people as well as their only criterion of a person's worth: keeping the law as they kept the law. Moreover, since none of the Temple leaders or Pharisees had believed Jesus, why should the police listen to him! Ironically, the next voice they heard was that of Nicodemus, a Pharisee who believed, who had seen in the signs that Jesus did someone who had clearly come from God.

A Story of Forgiveness

John 7:53–8:11 may be hard to find, depending on your edition of the Bible. It could be in a footnote or perhaps bracketed off from the rest of the text. That is because this story, the woman caught in adultery, is known as a "floating pericope" (*puh-ri-kuh-pee*; a term scholars use to refer to a unit of Scripture), which means that in the first collections of Jesus' teachings and stories about Jesus, it was not clear where this story belonged. It was, for a while, placed in Luke's Gospel because of Luke's interest in stories about women. But it found its way (through the early church fathers) into John's Gospel, and there it has stayed. It is a powerful story, showing the nature and character of Jesus in a beautiful way. It is written with the simple elegance of John's Gospel.

Jesus is teaching early in the morning at the Temple in Jerusalem. The Pharisees and scribes catch and drag to him a woman taken in adultery. They place her right in front of Jesus and the crowd that was listening to him. According to John's account, they wanted to trap him, unmasking him as a lawbreaker. They could not care less about the woman. They had zero compassion for her, zero interest in her need for forgiveness. She was a pawn in their game, a tool to catch Jesus. And so she stood there, perhaps half-dressed, in front of her neighbors, shivering, humiliated, not daring to look up. To get a feel for what she was going through, imagine yourself dragged out in front of your apartment or house with all your neighbors and friends watching, while the worst thing you've ever done in your life was being told to one and all!

The Pharisees remind Jesus of the Mosaic law about stoning adulterers. (That law applied to the man as well, but the Pharisees in this instance obviously weren't concerned about fairness.) There they stand, the righteous law-keepers, demanding that the law be kept—demanding the death penalty. They know that Rome forbade them to carry out a death penalty; so if Jesus should agree with them, they can accuse him of going against Rome.

Over against them sits Jesus. He bends down; he writes in the dirt with his finger. We can speculate as to what Jesus wrote, but no one knows. Personally, I think he was doodling, not looking at them in order to compose himself and to keep his anger in check. He looks up and says, "Whoever hasn't sinned should throw the first stone" (8:7). As Jesus again doodles in the dirt, they all leave in silence. He can hear the stones hitting the ground. The elders go first—they'd been around the block too many times to account themselves sinless. Then the young guys. No one is left but Jesus and the woman. "Woman, where are they? Is there no one to condemn you?" (8:10). "No one, sir" (8:11a). "Neither do I condemn you. Go, and from now on, don't sin anymore" (8:11bc).

That's the way God keeps the law, with compassion and forgiveness and a new beginning. *If you want to talk about the law of God, the church* fathers may have thought as they placed this story here in John, *this is the way to talk about it. Here is the nature of God revealed!*

This is a look at what it means to be set free from sin. It is a matter of the grace of God. "Therefore, if the Son makes you free, you really will be free" (John 8:36). In the story, Jesus does not ask the woman if she is repentant. He frees her with his love, and then he enjoins her not to do this sin again. Freedom from sin is a restored relationship with God: "Neither do I condemn you." This freedom to become the person you were created to be is offered to everyone without exception: to the inquiring Pharisee, Nicodemus; to the woman at the well and the woman caught in adultery; to the crowds at the festival; and to Jesus' opponents. No preconditions, no list of laws kept or deeds done. The freedom to be truly alive is based not on our goodness, but on God's.

Most people have heard the words "Then you will know the truth, and the truth will set you free" (John 8:32). They are even engraved on arches at the entrances to some universities, as if "the truth" were knowledge about mathematics or biology. In John's Gospel, *truth* is a technical term. It refers to knowing the answers to three questions: Who is Jesus? Where did he come from? Where is he going? Jesus himself is the truth. To understand who Jesus is, is to know through him that "God is love" (1 John 4:8); that God is for us; that there is a new beginning; and that you matter.

About the Scripture

Technical Terms in John

John uses some terms in precise ways throughout his writings. In addition to *truth*, which always means the way God is revealed in Jesus, there are several others. *World* is the word reserved for the people who are outside the faith community, those who oppose God. *Hour* means the critical time when Jesus' sacrifice and resurrection will glorify God. *One another* means fellow Christians (as it does in the Synoptics). *Lifted up* is an allusion to the Crucifixion.

Serving the One Who Can Make Us Whole

What are the things that truly enslave you, things from which you need to be set free? It could be some addiction or compulsion. It could be a dark sense of guilt or unworthiness. It might be a desire for acceptance from someone who cannot give it. It might be an enslavement to money and possessions—things people sometimes use to convince themselves that they deserve a place on the planet. It could be control over others or power to get your way.

Everyone serves a master. It may be that your master is acceptance or control or any of a thousand things. All false masters are cruel masters. You can never be free; you can never do enough—unless you serve the one master who is able to make you whole, the one of whom the Anglican Book of Common Prayer speaks when it says, "whose service is perfect freedom." To be the servant of God is to be, as William Stringfellow put it, "free in obedience."

Why is there no place in Jesus' opponents for his word? What is taking up the space? For them, it may have been pride and judgmentalism and all those rules and laws they had memorized. For us, it may be a preoccupation with work, an overly busy life that measures its importance by how desperately it is overscheduled. Perhaps it is an obsession with striving to be good enough to win God's favor or a burden of guilt over past failures. When there is no place for Jesus' word, there is a desire to be done with him: "You look for an opportunity to kill me, because there is no place in you for my word" (John 8:37, NRSV). Jesus was bringing them what he had seen "in the Father's presence." What more could we possibly need? And still Jesus instructed his opponents, still holding open to them the freedom of life lived in God: "As for you, you should do what you have heard from the Father" (8:38, NRSV). There was still time for them; they only needed to listen to the Father, to hear the message that is Jesus. It is possible to be free from every cruel, misery-making master and to serve God. One only has to hear Christ's invitation. Keeping every letter of the law cannot save because "being saved" has to do with a living relationship, not with performing certain works in certain ways. It has to do with embodying the love of God in your life, not keeping score of how many laws you keep. Keeping the law without God's love and compassion is worthless. It means exactly nothing.

Live the Story

Look seriously at the way you are living your life. What is its driving force? Why do you get up in the morning? When all is said and done, who is your master? Many "church people" are rule-keepers. They see keeping rules and laws as a way of knowing whether they are following God or not. That presents a huge danger. We have seen that the Pharisees and scribes were great rule-keepers, but that didn't necessarily make them close to God.

Life with God is not about keeping laws. Life with God, now and in the life to come, is a matter of embracing who God is, celebrating God's nature revealed in Jesus, becoming more and more like him as we live joined to him—branches on a vine, vessels for living water. It's not in the rote keeping of laws that life is found; it's in knowing God, the God we see in Jesus.

Are you trying to be "good enough" for God to love you? Are you trying to keep as many laws as you can so that you will know you are following God? Do you pride yourself on being just a bit better than some others you could name? How well are you listening to Jesus' description of God? Jesus has a warning: Your law-keeping won't work. And he has an invitation: "All who are thirsty should come to me!" (7:37).

5.

Who Is the God Whom Jesus Reveals?

John 6:35; 8:12; 9:5; 10:7, 9, 11, 14; 11:25-26; 14:6; 15:1
John 4:26; 6:20; 8:24, 28, 58; 13:19; 18:5, 6, 8

Claim Your Story

If you were asked to describe the nature of God, what would you say? Do you immediately think of God as a judge or a bookkeeper, keeping track of your every fault? Would you describe God as remote, far above the universe somewhere? Is God the one who reminds you that you never are quite good enough to pass muster? Or is God endlessly indulgent, forgiving everything? Is God some "unmoved mover," creator of all that is but not available to people? Where do you get your ideas about God? Leftover thinking from childhood? Televangelists? Concepts from other religions? Cultural beliefs? Is your God the God of Scripture?

J. B. Phillips in 1961 wrote a little book called *Your God Is Too Small.* The chapter titles are provocative: Resident Policeman, Parental Hangover, Grand Old Man, Meek-and-Mild, Absolute Perfection, Heavenly Bosom, God-in-a-Box, Managing Director, Second-Hand God, Perennial Grievance, Pale Galilean, Projected Image, Assorted. Most of them speak for themselves. Many, many people invent a god out of bits and pieces— things from their thinking as children, ideas from different religions, popular notions, assumptions. Some people use their self-invented gods as reasons to reject the Christian faith, assuming that the God they have invented is the God of Scripture. One of the saddest outcomes of these self-invented gods is that people sometimes spend their lives trying to appease the god of their own invention; and in wasting their time and energy on these invented gods, they miss out on a relationship with the God who is revealed in Scripture.

Enter the Bible Story

As we have been discovering, John's Gospel is all about answering three questions, one of which is "Who is Jesus?" The reason John sees this as an important question is that Jesus reveals the nature of God: "Whoever has seen me has seen the Father" (John 14:9b). Jesus constantly points past himself to "the Father." The enfleshed self-expression of God is the subject of this Gospel.

Nothing makes that clearer than the "I am" sayings of Jesus, which are found only in the Fourth Gospel. There are seven such sayings that end with a noun describing Jesus and thereby give insight into the nature of God. In addition, there are nine others that do not have specific nouns attached. It is these verses that will help us see that the Scriptures do not deal with some nebulous, subjective idea of "God" but rather are quite specific as to who God is.

Across the Testaments

Metaphors for God

The "description" of the nature of God does not begin in the New Testament. God is described in many specific ways in the Old Testament. The word most often used to describe God in the Old Testament is not a word that talks about the vengeance of God, as many might suppose. The most-used term to describe God is *hesed*, "loving-kindness." God is also described as our rock, our fortress, our shepherd, light, salvation, a mother bear, strength, shield, king, and many others. God's name is revealed in Exodus 3. Moses, hoping to get out of God's demand that he go to Egypt to confront Pharaoh, asks God what God's name is—sure that God will not reveal it, as he had not revealed it to Jacob (Genesis 32:29). Much to Moses' chagrin, God reveals his sacred name, YHWH (Yahweh). This is usually translated "I AM" or "I AM WHO I AM." "I AM," then, is the holy name of the one God, a name too sacred for pious Jews to pronounce.

The Incarnation of "I Am"

The first group of "I am" sayings does not have descriptive nouns. In the English translations of these, Jesus says "I am he" or "It is I" or "I Am." These statements are unusual constructions in the original Greek. They are statements that, instead of using metaphors for the nature of God, state that Jesus simply is the incarnation of the nature of God—the God of the Old Testament, Yahweh, the I AM. The most obvious of these is John 8:58: "Before Abraham was, I Am." It comes at the end of an acrimonious debate between Jesus and the Jewish leaders. There is really no other way to interpret this than as a statement of divinity, specifically referring to the God of the Old Testament. Jesus' opponents think so; for as soon as he says it, they attempt to stone him for blasphemy (8:59)! In John 4:26, when the Samaritan woman is trying to figure out if Jesus could be Messiah, Jesus responds, "I Am." In John 6:20, when the disciples see him walking on the waves, he calms their fears by saying, "It is I" (which is the same construction in Greek). It is clear that Jesus means that to watch what he says and does is to see clearly the nature of I AM. In John 8:24 and 28, Jesus makes it clear that to identify what people see in Jesus with the I AM is crucial. Without understanding who Jesus is, they will not be able to hear and understand the message of life that he brings and is.

In John 13:19 and in 18:5, 6, 8 (translated as "I am he"), there is a connection with Jesus' suffering and death. In John, this is the hour of Jesus' glorification. It is in this that the self-giving love of God is displayed in all its glory. This loving sacrifice is the great I AM giving all for God's children. In the arrest scene, the opponents of Christ fall to the ground when he pronounces the holy name (18:6). Jesus reveals the God of the Old Testament—I AM.

The metaphors attached to the seven "I am" sayings of Jesus that end with nouns are:

- I am the Bread of Life
- I am the Light of the World
- I am the Door of the Sheepfold
- I am the Good Shepherd

- I am the Resurrection and the Life
- I am the Way, the Truth, and the Life
- I am the True Vine

Remember that Jesus, as always, points beyond himself to God the Father (another metaphor) whenever he describes himself. We could almost read these sayings like this: "I am: the bread of life." All these metaphors speak of the nature of God as it has to do with God's relationship to humanity. God is the source of our real life (bread); God is our guide (light); God is our safe passage into the world (door of the sheepfold); God is our protector (shepherd); God is our victory over death (resurrection and life); God in Christ is our example for living the truly human life (the way and the truth); and God is the source of life and the one who makes us able to be truly human (the vine). But these descriptions are not cut-and-dried; they are many-faceted. Every time you revisit one, you can find new insight.

There are many ways you might summarize these descriptions, but it's hard to see how any of them could be morphed into "vengeful judge" or "remote and unmoved." The least that we could say about these seven metaphors is that they describe a God who is present and active on behalf of God's human creatures. This is the God who gives us a future. This is a God who is "for us." This is a God who is light years better than any god you may have been inventing for yourself.

To watch Jesus live the authentic human life is to have our best selves modeled for us. To see Jesus give himself to all kinds of people in all circumstances is to see what the nature of God looks like in human flesh. When Jesus utters one of these sayings, it is attached to the man who lived a particular life in a particular way.

This group of "I am" sayings also defines God in terms of promises: to give life and guidance, protection and companionship. It's like the man says: "It's all good!" This is the God who is present and will remain with his people. No wonder it's called "good news"! This is something to celebrate, but sometimes things get in the way of our hearing the news. Such was true of those to whom Jesus first brought this incarnate nature of God.

The Bread of Life

In John 6:30-31, the crowds demand a sign such as the manna from heaven described in Exodus 16. Jesus declares, "I am the bread of life" (John 6:35). He expands on that declaration in verses 48-51:

> I am the bread of life. Your ancestors ate manna in the wilderness and they died. This is the bread that comes down from heaven so that whoever eats from it will never die. I am the living bread that came down from heaven. Whoever eats this bread will live forever, and the bread that I will give for the life of the world is my flesh.

The people respond by arguing among themselves (6:60). Those who heard Jesus' words on a literal plane, including many of Jesus' numerous disciples, were disgusted. As with Nicodemus and the Samaritan woman, hearing only the literal and failing to understand who Jesus is spiritually leads to an inability to see God in what Jesus says and does. If they had understood that Jesus was the incarnation of God's Word, they would have heard a message of life and self-giving love from God. Were they afraid to hear? We wonder what might have kept them from hearing good news. Of course, even with the perspective of 2,000 years, often we do not hear either!

The Light of the World

The audience is different in John 8:12, where Jesus declares, "I am the light of the world. Whoever follows me won't walk in darkness but will have the light of life." In this case it is the Pharisees who hear (or fail to hear) Jesus' pronouncement. They had already decided against him. Instead of disputing his claim, they go after technicalities. They try to use Jesus' own words against him: "If I testify about myself, my testimony isn't true" (5:31). Jesus contended that his word is valid because God the Father stands with him. The Pharisees again show their lack of understanding by asking Jesus, "Where is your Father?" (8:19). Jesus had offered his opponents the "light of life"; but they had not even heard the invitation, since they were preoccupied with countering Jesus' every statement. People who instantly counter every statement with a criticism or contradiction are not even trying to hear.

In John 9:5, Jesus declares, "While I am in the world, I am the light of the world." Jesus certainly meant that he makes it possible for any and all to see the path God would have them walk. He may also mean that in seeing Jesus, they see a measuring rod by which they can measure their own closeness to God (see John 3:20-21).

The Good Shepherd

John 10:11-16 presents us with a vision of Jesus that is beloved by most Christians: the Good Shepherd. Again, the connection to God—in addition to the "I am" statements—should have been clear to Jesus' first hearers. For in Ezekiel 34, in an excoriation of Israel's kings—bad shepherds who destroy the flock they were supposed to protect—God declared that he himself would be Israel's shepherd. God pledged to be the good shepherd who would protect the sheep and be just. Jesus' hearers could not fail to make the connection. Here, a battered and occupied people were rehearing the promise of the Good Shepherd. Jesus is also the gate through which the sheep safely pass and which is their protection through the dark night (10:7-10).

Some people responded to Jesus' voice as sheep to their loving shepherd. Others did not. Again and again, John uses people's reactions to Jesus as the way to measure their relationship to God. The response was mixed. The people did not understand him, so Jesus expanded on the topic. He said that he had the power to lay down his life and take it up again (10:17-18). It was at this point that the people began to dispute with one another. Some called him crazy, while other people could not believe that the one who opened the eyes of the blind could be anything but authentic (10:19-21).

The Resurrection and the Life

Chapter 11 is the story of the raising of Lazarus from the dead. It is the seventh and last sign in the Gospel. It will serve as the reason for the presence of great crowds in Jerusalem on Palm Sunday (12:18). Lazarus' sister, Martha, seems to scold Jesus. As far as she was concerned, Jesus showed up late—too late. Death was king, and death had won. Jesus responds to her with the words, "Your brother will rise again." Martha's reply may startle some modern-day people: "I know." This was not a news flash for Martha. Martha believed what the Pharisees believed: "I know that he will rise in the resurrection on the last day" (11:24). This was a growing belief among first-century Jews.

But Jesus meant more: "I am the resurrection and the life" (11:25). Death is not the immovable object in this life or the next. The resurrection is not simply a future event. The resurrection is the power of God over all the enemies of God's people—now and in the future. There are plenty of walking dead around us. There are people simply going through the motions, people who fear everything around them, people for whom every day is pain in the heart and mind. These people can experience resurrection now, for God wills life for God's people. The promise is the destruction of all that stunts life now and the destruction of the death that would try to separate us from God forever. This is the God who is the author of life, whose nature is incarnate in Jesus.

The Way, the Truth, and the Life

The "I am" saying in 14:6 is very difficult to interpret. Jesus declares himself to be "the way, the truth, and the life." Those words are used many, many times in our Scriptures and have a variety of interpretations. "The way" often means a path to a destination. But it can also mean a "way of life." Is Jesus the way to the truth and the life? Since Jesus declares that he is the truth and he is the life, perhaps "way" should be taken as meaning what Jesus is in his life and actions. These words all come together in Jesus.

Some people insist that the words "No one comes to the Father except through me" mean that unless one professes Christianity, one is doomed. Even if John, in his ongoing war of words with the Jewish leaders of his day (some 45–60 years after Jesus), meant the words to carry this connotation, they can be seen in other ways—ways that fit in better with what we see of Jesus in other Gospels and in other places in John. In Matthew 25:31-46, Jesus clearly states that those who do the works of love without knowing him are welcomed by the Father. In Mark 12:34, he tells a Jewish scribe who sees clearly that love of God and neighbor is key, "You aren't far from God's kingdom." Doing the works of love is the crucial point. Remember that in John's Gospel to believe means to act. Jesus' words challenge us to live not as the judge of others, but as a pathway for them to a welcoming and loving God.

The Vine and the Branches

The last of the seven "I am" sayings is found in John 15:1-8, the metaphor of the vine and branches. It becomes abundantly clear here that faith in Jesus consists not of a list of instructions and laws that we can take and walk away with, living the Christian life under our own steam. Rather, we need the life of Christ coursing through us in order to live as God intends us to live—loving God and neighbor. We can't do it on our own: "Without me, you can't do anything" (15:5). Jesus does not mean that we can't do the chores of everyday life. He means that by ourselves we cannot bear the fruit that God wants from us. This fruit is the multiplication of the love of God in the world. If the rooted vine is Christ, then what grows on the vine will be Christ—the incarnate love of God in the world. This is an intimate and powerful relationship! It is this relationship that enables people to bear fruit for God.

Live the Story

John's Gospel won't allow you to drag out any old definition or description of God and then call yourself a follower of Jesus. The God of Jesus is not generic in either the Old or New Testaments. The "I am" statements show us a God who is for us, close to us, a God who calls us to a certain way of living: a life connected to this very specific God. This God, revealed in Jesus Christ, calls us into a relationship with God that begins now and does not end.

Is this the God you have in mind when you think of God or when you pray? How much of what you believe about God has its roots in the Scriptures? Where does your God come from? Have you been confronted by the God whom Jesus shows us? How does the God whom Jesus shows us affect the way you feel or think or pray or act?

6.

To Be a Disciple of Jesus Christ

John 12:1-8, 12-19; 13:1-17, 31-35

Claim Your Story

Do you identify yourself as a disciple of Jesus Christ? If so, what do you mean by that? The word *disciple* means "someone who believes and helps to spread the doctrine of another."[1] A disciple is also a student, someone who listens to the ideas of a teacher. Both of these descriptions can be pretty safe activities. Spreading doctrine is not hard to do. It is not usually thought of as a dangerous assignment. Agreeing with a set of ideas means nothing more than that—just agreeing. What can you identify in your life that demonstrates that you are a disciple of Jesus? In what areas do you feel inadequate? What would you like to improve?

If you do not designate yourself a disciple, yet you are reading this study, what do you think is holding you back? Do you think that you just don't know enough yet? Are you waiting for a feeling or emotion to tell you it's time to declare yourself? Do some of the so-called disciples of Jesus that you have seen and heard put you off? Are you afraid you are not good enough? Perhaps you don't want others to think that you are what is meant when the word *disciple* is used.

What does it mean to be a disciple of Jesus Christ? Is it a matter of knowing the right ideas, thinking the right thoughts, feeling the right feelings? How would you know if you were a disciple?

Enter the Bible Story

As Jesus' hour rapidly approaches, he focuses attention on what it means to live as his disciple. Jesus of Nazareth will soon leave the picture. It is the disciples, empowered by the Holy Spirit, who will become the representation of Christ in the world. They must be made ready. Any and all who would be Jesus' disciples need to contemplate what discipleship means.

A Picture of a True Disciple

Chapter 12 opens with a picture of a true disciple: Mary. She understands who Jesus is. John the Baptist had said that he was "not worthy to untie his sandal straps" (John 1:27). Mary showed that she understood that kind of relationship by taking it upon herself to do for Jesus a deed that was truly humbling: anointing his feet. She understood where she ranked compared to the Son of God! In two Gospels—John and Luke—Mary is lifted up as the disciple who does things right. In Luke 10:40-42, while Martha was rushing around in the kitchen, Mary was at the feet of Jesus. She was listening, learning who Jesus was. Martha's complaint that Mary's place was in the kitchen was countered by Jesus as he defended Mary: "Mary has chosen the better part, which will not be taken away from her" (10:42, NRSV). Not only did she see who Jesus was when some others did not, in John 12:1-8 she acted on that knowledge, honoring him with an outpouring of devotion that was generous, uncalculated, and not concerned with cost—only with worship.

Jesus interpreted her action as preparation for his death (12:7). While one never anointed with oil or perfume the feet of the living, it could be done during the anointing of a corpse. The coming death of Jesus and the depth of the disciples' understanding are seen in tandem in this last part of the Gospel. Because of Jesus' death, the disciples must understand clearly who they are and what their role is to be. But it was difficult for them to hear the message. There was a terrible tension between beholding the glory of Christ and the coming death of the Messiah. Who could accept what was about to happen?

Judas' example stands in stark contrast to Mary's. According to John, he mouthed pious words about the poor but saw Mary's action only as the loss of an opportunity to steal from Jesus—if only Mary had sold the perfume and given the proceeds to the common purse (12:4-6)! Judas attempted to make Mary look bad while trying to appear virtuous himself. Jesus sees through the duplicity easily and, as he had in Luke, defends Mary: "Leave her alone" (12:7). Mary's anointing of Jesus' feet as a sign of her love and devotion will soon be echoed by Jesus himself as he washes the disciples' feet, teaching them the appropriate attitude of one Christian toward another (Chapter 13).

Jesus as the True King

Following the anointing, Jesus goes to face those who would kill him. In 12:12-19, he acts out a living parable of sorts to show the world (the crowds who came for the Passover and those who followed him after having seen the raising of Lazarus) who he is. A king who was not yet in possession of a city entered it only on a warhorse and with a contingent of armed soldiers. He did not have control of the city. A king, however, who had already conquered a city could ride in on a donkey, with no military guard, showing that he was confident of his place as the one in control. John quotes Zechariah 9:9 in 12:15. John, with his love of irony, puts the truth of the event into the mouths of Jesus' opponents as the Pharisees say to each other, "See! You've accomplished nothing! Look! The whole world is following him!" (12:19). As the true king, Jesus had no need to throw his weight around or to threaten violence. His power is the power of self-giving love. That love brings those who accept him to their knees in thanksgiving and in service.

A Demonstration of Servanthood

Later that same week, the disciples see the Son of God on his knees, acting as a slave before this imperfect group, a sight that Peter cannot bear (John 13:1-17). The footwashing scene, rather than the Last Supper, is highlighted in John's Maundy Thursday text. John incorporated the words concerning the body and blood of Jesus into Chapter 6. He chose

About the Christian Faith

Maundy Thursday

Maundy Thursday commemorates the evening before Jesus' death. This was the evening in which, according to the Synoptics, Jesus instituted the Last Supper (also called Holy Communion and the Eucharist; Matthew 26:17-30; Mark 14:12-26; Luke 22:7-23). The Last Supper was Jesus' reinterpretation of the Passover seder in terms of his own sacrifice. John records the footwashing and Jesus' new commandment that his followers must love one another (13:1-11, 34-35). It is probably best to put these two events together in order to get the real flavor of the evening. Jesus' sacrifice, his giving of himself for the disciples as made visible in Communion, leads to his commandment that as he has loved, so must they love. This is his commandment for all who call themselves Jesus' disciples.

here to showcase the call to servanthood as the centerpiece of the section on discipleship.

Peter's protest about what Jesus was about to do for him was rebuffed by Jesus (13:8). If Peter is to be a disciple of Jesus, he must receive and depend on the self-giving love of God as the power behind existence. If Peter refused, he would be refusing what power means for Jesus. He must participate as an acceptance of the truth about God. He must also participate in order to show that he is a true servant who will serve his brothers and sisters in Christ. So must every disciple of Jesus Christ acknowledge by action that our Master showed us how to serve.

We should remember that Judas was among those to have his feet washed. Can we imagine the tension there as Jesus washed the feet—in perhaps a last offer of love—of the one who within the hour would turn him over to the police? Loving your enemies begins at home!

Jesus tells the disciples to wash each other's feet (13:14). "Each other" serves as a technical term in the New Testament, meaning "fellow Christians." It was important for them not to take this instruction literally. Jesus' action meant much more than a call to perform one more ritual. Christians were to be each other's servants, doing for a fellow Christian whatever was needed. The world would then look to this fellowship of faith and see there a picture of how life is lived in the kingdom of God. The church is designed to be a foretaste of the Kingdom that is yet to be, an example that draws people to it (see Isaiah 2:2-3). But even beyond that, the church is to be the residence of the Holy Spirit. This is how Paul can call the church "the body of Christ" (e.g., 1 Corinthians 12:27). The church is to be the living representation of Christ to the world. When members of a congregation act in unholy ways toward each other, therefore, it is a much worse offense than a slight to an individual. It is a misrepresentation of the nature of Jesus Christ.

John 13:31-35 begins with a statement by Jesus announcing that he "has been glorified, and God has been glorified in him." Glory belongs to God. Glory is the manifestation of the greatness of God. As Jesus stands poised on the brink of obeying God to the very death, he announces that God "has been glorified in him." Jesus' obedience to self-giving love had made the love of God visible. In the Book of Hebrews, the author seeks to explain the relationship of Christ to God the Father. He writes, "The Son is the light of God's glory and the imprint of God's being" (Hebrews 1:3a). Finally, Christ in his act of obedience cannot be separated from the true nature of God any more than we could separate the sun from its shining. In who Jesus is and what Jesus is doing, God is revealed for us.

A New Commandment

The theme of Jesus as the enfleshed nature of God is heard in three ways in this text: in the statement about glory; in the reminder that the disciples cannot go where Jesus is going (he came from God); and in the giving of a commandment. Only God gives commandments. This "new commandment" is the source of the name "Maundy Thursday." *Maundy* is from the Latin for "command." I have always thought that this instruction to the church rises to the level of a sacrament, since it was clearly commanded by Christ as something Christians must do and something in which Christ himself participated. I suppose that it's not a sacrament because there is no one "outward sign" for loving one another—or rather, there are too many signs! Be that as it may, the message should be clear to Christians that their relationship to others in the faith community is sacred. This commandment should be chiseled over the entry to every church building, as well as on the heart of every person of faith.

The way that many people in local congregations treat each other is seen in a new light when laid beside the new commandment. Christ said, "This is how everyone will know that you are my disciples, when you love each other" (John 13:35). Too often, people in the church declare their love of humanity while treating their fellow church members rudely, thoughtlessly, and sometimes with outright contempt. They talk about loving everyone in general yet do not show that love in the particular! How easy to "love" an idealized, faraway group of people one has never met—African orphans, for example—while at the same time gossiping about the person one sits behind in worship every Sunday! In the words of the great twentieth-century theologian Linus from the Peanuts cartoons, "I love humanity, it's people I can't stand."

Some folks will maintain that they love God with all their heart, soul, mind, and strength yet ignore the needs of their brothers and sisters in the faith and sometimes wish them ill. The new commandment says that we cannot call ourselves disciples of Jesus Christ if we are not doing the works of love for one another. (Remember, "love" in John's Gospel is the works of love, not an emotion.) Nor are we being honest when we declare our love for God but despise a fellow Christian. John himself puts this more eloquently in his first letter to the church: "Those who say, 'I love God,' and hate their brothers or sisters, are liars; for those who do not love a brother or sister whom they have seen, cannot love God whom they have not seen. The commandment we have from him is this: those who love God must love their brothers and sisters also" (1 John 4:20-21, NRSV). In this context, "brothers and sisters" refers to brothers and sisters in the faith. It is likely that John here is referencing the new commandment given on Maundy Thursday.

One reason for doing the works of love for each other is to attract the world to God. In the early days of the church, the Romans took notice of how the Christians cared for one another's needs. What do people notice about us today? Christianity is not charged with making a club for insiders. Its purpose is to show the world what God's love is. It has been said that the church is the one institution that exists for those who don't belong to it!

In the church, nothing is done only for ourselves. People sometimes say that they don't feel like going to worship—as though they were only going for themselves. We don't show up at corporate worship just for ourselves; we attend in order to create the church for others. We go so that the stranger coming through the door for the first time in search of a relationship with God is not discouraged by the small number of worshipers but rather encouraged by the many. We go to keep the promise we made to the community to be present with them. We go to witness to our teens and children and to the unconvinced that something is here that should be noticed!

One of the most important things for members of the faith community to practice is remembering who they are in the church and why they are there. Jesus gives the church a way to do this. We can look back at the ways in which Jesus loved the first disciples and, by extension, us. His patience with their inability to see past the literal, his correction in love of their mistakes, his willingness to put up with their weaknesses, and his forgiveness of their betrayal all say something to us about Christ's expectations of our treatment of one another. His example was not limited to footwashing; it extends to his entire way of living.

Live the Story

In Luke 6:46, Jesus says, "Why do you call me 'Lord, Lord' and don't do what I say?" In other words, we are not Christ's servants if we are not doing the works of love. Extensive research has indicated that today's younger adults will most likely not approach the church through the sanctuary door. They have little interest in what we say until they have seen what we do. They will first join the church's Habitat project, homeless outreach, hunger march, tutoring ministry, or the like before they show much interest in our message. The old way of coming to church to hear first is dying, and perhaps a healthier way of approaching the church is taking the ascendancy.

What is the scope of your discipleship? Have you gotten past "Lord, Lord"? Have you not only heard but also acted upon what you have heard? Discipleship goes on in the head and the heart, but it is true discipleship only when it is translated into love for one another and love for whomever is put in our path. The world does not want to hear your doctrines and beliefs if it cannot see them lived out. The life that can't be ignored is the life that lives for others.

Maybe you've been waiting for a warm feeling of Christ's presence to make you into a disciple. But that is rarely the way it happens. More often it is as Dr. Albert Schweitzer—the Mother Teresa of the 1950's and 1960's—said:

> He comes to us as One unknown, without a name, as of old, by the lakeside, He came to those men who knew Him not. He speaks to us the same word: "Follow thou me!" and sets us to the tasks which He has to fulfil for our time. He commands. And to those who obey Him, whether they be wise or simple, He will reveal Himself in the toils, the conflicts, the sufferings which they shall pass through in His fellowship, and, as an ineffable mystery, they shall learn in their own experience Who He is.[2]

For Schweitzer and for John, to be a disciple is to give yourself, with Jesus, to the works of love and thus to glorify God.

[1] From *http://wordnetweb.princeton.edu/perl/webwn?s=disciple*.
[2] From *The Quest of the Historical Jesus* (Macmillan, 1968); page 403.

7.

The Holy Spirit Creates and Sustains the Church

John 14:15-29; 15:26-27; 16:5-15; 17:1-26

Claim Your Story

The church of Jesus Christ is not like a grocery store, although many churchgoers seem to treat it that way. In a grocery store you presume that someone else has prepared everything so that you merely have to go there, pick what you want, pay for it, and leave. Your interest is not in helping all the other people in the store find what they need. You are concerned only with your own grocery list. You may or may not see people you know and speak to them, but that is not why you go to the grocery store. You go for yourself and those for whom you prepare food. If the store should close, it may be inconvenient; but you'll soon find another place to shop.

Some people go to church on Sunday with precisely the same attitude. For them, the church is something that has been put together by someone else. They have nothing to do with making sure everything needed is available. They come to church to get something for themselves; witness the common complaint "I didn't get anything out of that service." Many times, people in church only speak to those they happen to know; the strangers and visitors are not their concern. Having paid for what they came for, these churchgoers leave. Should the church fail and close, or fail to provide the goods they're used to, they will simply go to another.

When viewed from the perspective of the self-centered churchgoer, the church is nothing more than a philosophical club or a historical society, a place where those who believe the same religious doctrine gather to hear it once more and then leave. This has so little to do with what God created the church for that it's startling! It leaves the church a dead thing, connected only to the distant past. If there is any work to be done at all, it is to convince others of the correctness of their doctrine or history and so add to the number of churchgoers.

Have you ever tended to treat the church of Jesus Christ as a grocery store? When you go to church, is it all about you—what you need, what you expect, what makes you comfortable? Well, turn loose of that shopping cart and put away the list. It's time to see the church more as Jesus envisioned it.

Enter the Bible Story

Chapters 14–16 in John's Gospel constitute Jesus' farewell address. He speaks in this section only to those who were disciples, to those who were gathered in the upper room. There may well have been many more there than the twelve apostles. Jesus' focus is on what the disciples must do when he is no longer there in the flesh to lead them. He assures them that though physically absent, he would still be with them and in an even more powerful way. In John 14:15-29, Jesus promises the faithful that the "Companion," "the Spirit of Truth," would be sent by God to lead the disciples. In John as in Luke and in Paul's letters, it is the Spirit of God that will empower the church (see Luke 24:49; Acts 2:1-4; 1 Corinthians 12:12-13).

The first thing we discover about the church is that it is far more than a collection of like-minded individuals chugging along under their own steam. The church's life and vitality come from the indwelling Holy Spirit. The Spirit is identified in various ways in the New Testament: as the Holy Spirit; the Spirit; the Spirit of God; the Spirit of Christ; the Spirit of Jesus; the Advocate; the Helper; and here, Companion and the Spirit of Truth.

The current passage looks to the time when Jesus' followers would face persecution for their discipleship: "The time is coming when those who kill you will think that they are doing a service to God" (16:2). This should not come as a shock to followers. If "the world" rejected Christ, it would also stand against his followers; that is one important reason why the Spirit is given. The word *Companion* translates the Greek *paraklete* (pronounced like *parakeet*, only with an "l"). The Greek verb from which the noun Paraclete is derived means "to call to one's aid." The King James Version translates it "Comforter"; the RSV says "Counselor"; the NRSV has "Advocate" or "Helper." The Paraclete will be with the church and stand with the church "forever" (14:16). The word *you* in 14:15 is plural. It is the fellowship of Christ's followers that is being addressed. As a man, Jesus could not remain with the church forever. But the Spirit of Christ, sent by God—and by Christ (16:7)—can and will.

As its constant Companion, what will the Spirit do in and for the church? The Spirit's first job is to teach the community of faith (14:26) and remind them of everything that Jesus had said. It is the teaching of the Spirit and the words of Jesus that guide the life of the church. In 15:26-27, Jesus says that the Paraclete will testify about him and make it possible for his followers to testify as well, especially in times of persecution. In 16:7-8, Jesus tells the disciples, "It is better for you that I go away. If I don't go away, the Companion won't come to you." The Paraclete can be with the church, wherever it is, in a way that Jesus of Nazareth cannot. The Paraclete, in a passage difficult to understand, is also to "show the world it was wrong about sin, righteousness, and judgment" (16:8). The Paraclete stands against the evil of the world and makes it possible for the church to do the same.

It is necessary for the follower of Christ then to ask, "In living a life where no one really attacks or challenges what I do, have I succumbed to the ways of the world? Do I get along too well with the world?" When people of faith speak truth to power, they almost always pay a personal price. Those who protested the evil of segregation in the 1950's and 60's were beaten, imprisoned, ostracized, and in some cases killed. They spoke the word against the world, and the world made them pay. When the people of the church do not rock any boats, are they really following Christ? How can we be comfortable in the world and follow Jesus at the

About the Christian Faith

Empowered by the Spirit

The Apostles' Creed: "I believe in the Holy Spirit."

The Nicene Creed: "We believe in the Holy Spirit, the Lord, the giver of Life, who proceeds from the Father and the Son."

A Statement of Faith of the Korean Methodist Church: "We believe in the Holy Spirit, God present with us for guidance, for comfort, and for strength."

A Modern Affirmation: "We believe in the Holy Spirit as the divine presence in our lives, whereby we are kept in perpetual remembrance of the truth of Christ, and find strength and help in time of need."[1]

same time? Jesus promised his own presence through the Paraclete in order to give his followers strength to stand against the world. Does the church trust that promise? Does the church today see it as an important promise?

These passages make it clear that Christ expected and expects his church to get into trouble by standing against the world's evil. The membership vows of The United Methodist Church reflect this as well:

Do you renounce the spiritual forces of wickedness,
>   reject the evil powers of this world,
>   and repent of your sin?
I do.
Do you accept the freedom and power God gives you
>   to resist evil, injustice, and oppression
>   in whatever forms they present themselves?
I do.[2]

First, one is asked to "renounce the spiritual forces of wickedness," which I take to mean powers such as hatred, racism, division, gossip, and whatever other powers people use to hurt others. After you relinquish those evil powers, the next question asks if you will accept a new power—the "power God gives you," which I take to mean the power of the Holy Spirit, which has been given to the faith community. If you say "I do," you suddenly find yourself in the resistance—resisting evil, injustice, and oppression. Make no mistake about it, these things do not like being resisted! So we end up with a church that looks less and less like a grocery store and more and more like a community with marching orders that take them into the world!

The church is called to defend the oppressed, whether it be those who are economically or racially oppressed or those who are being physically and emotionally oppressed. Justice means taking on systems that work against groups of people. Evil can be thought of as all those things that keep people from drawing close to God, that keep them from becoming the people God created them to be. A study of the church's membership vows may be a good place for a local congregation to start thinking about what it means to be the church.

There's an old saying that was meant as a warning to clergy: "You've gone from preachin' to meddlin'," meaning that the preacher was beginning to step on someone's toes. The church is called to "meddle" with injustice, evil, and oppression; and it is given God's own presence to do so. And the church, when it is being the church, expects evil to push back. Those who are comfortable with the way things are feel seriously threatened by any group that attempts to change the status quo. Thankfully, the Paraclete is with the church!

Jesus' Special Prayer for the Church

John placed what has been called "the high priestly prayer" immediately following the farewell address. The prayer is called that because in it Jesus intercedes for the church—the community of all those who follow Christ. It takes up all of John 17. There are three emphases in the prayer: the work of Jesus Christ, the disciples who are being sent by Christ into the world, and the faith community of the future that comes into existence through the word of the disciples.

In the first section, Jesus sums up what he has accomplished with the new faith community: "Now they know that everything you have given me comes from you. This is because I gave them the words that you gave me, and they received them. They truly understood that I came from you, and they believed that you sent me" (17:7-8). Knowing where Jesus came from makes it possible truly to hear what Jesus is saying and to know that his words are from God. Jesus, then, has come to create this community— the church.

In the second section, Jesus prays specifically for his current disciples— not just the Twelve, but the great body of believers. This part of the prayer asks for protection for the community. Not protection from persecution— Jesus had already told them they would be persecuted—but protection from "the evil one" (17:15; the word can also be translated "evil"). Evil is the power to make them stop following God. The disciples must be protected from denying their faith. They are in danger because "as you sent me into the world, so I have sent them into the world" (17:18). The purpose of the church is to go into the world and do what Jesus did. Why? "For God so loved the world that he gave his only Son, so that everyone who believes in him won't perish but will have eternal life" (John 3:16). Just as Jesus was sent into the world to love it, so is the church. That grocery store thing is looking more and more pointless! Remember: " 'Eternal life' is not a gift of immortality or a future life in heaven, but a life shaped by the knowledge of God as revealed in Jesus."[3] The church is so to live in the world that the world will see the truth of God revealed in them, and seeing it, will choose to follow the God revealed in Christ. After a local congregation is finished studying their membership vows, they might take as their next study and discussion question, "How is the church to love the world?"

The final part of the prayer finds Jesus praying for us—the church of the future! "I'm not praying only for them but also for those who believe in me because of their [the disciples'] word. I pray they will be one" (17:20-21). Jesus uses the concept of being "one" in the same way in which he used it in John 10:30: one in unity of purpose and of knowledge through Jesus. Through Jesus we come to know who God is and, by extension, who we are called to be. This unity of faith and action will draw the world to Christ (as the Pharisees feared in John 12:19). The church in its proclamation and life is to show the truth of God's love to the world. The church is then to go out into that world and love it.

The faith community is intertwined with the Father and the Son: "I'm in them and you are in me so that they will be made perfectly one" (17:23a). The faith community is sanctified, made holy—that is, set aside for God's use—because of its knowledge of the truth: in seeing Christ, it is seeing the nature of God.

As Jesus made clear in the metaphor of the vine and the branches, the Christian community is alive only when it is connected to Christ; this connection is the Holy Spirit. The church that thinks it lives by the willpower of its members cuts itself off from its true source of life and power. This is the congregation that allows the finance committee to tell them whether a certain ministry that they feel called to take on is "possible." This is the congregation that, instead of gathering together for prayer and discernment, simply says, "We can't afford it" or "We're too small." This is the congregation that turns itself into a club for the current members and ignores or is even irritated by "outsiders." This is the congregation that turns into a "Safeway" or a "Winn-Dixie." A third question, then, that a congregation might want to get together to discuss might be, "When the congregation says they can't do something they feel God is calling them to do, what are they saying about the presence of the Holy Spirit?"

Live the Story

The Scriptures, both Old and New Testaments, know nothing of solitary religion. Israel was called into existence as a people to be "a light to the nations" (e.g., Isaiah 42:6; 49:6, NRSV). The word *nations* means about the same thing in the Old Testament as *world* does in John's Gospel. The church is called into the world to love the world and to demonstrate God's love in the internal workings of the Christian community. God has set us in community to be a microcosm of the Kingdom and has empowered it by God's Holy Spirit. But if a congregation does not believe that, if they have no real ecclesiology (a theology of the church), they will always fail to be what God in Christ created them to be.

What is your part in the faith community? Have you been trying to know God just for yourself? Have you seen faith as a personal and private experience that begins and ends with you? Have you bought into grocery store thinking? Where do you need to rethink your concept of the church?

If you are part of a congregation, what does the general feeling about its work seem to be? Is loving the world labeled as "mission work" and reserved for those who "like that sort of thing," or is the congregation's mission to love one another so they can love the world as Christ loves it?

If your congregation needs help in looking seriously at its purpose and the source of its power, what can you do to help move it in a new direction? Where do discussions and faithful actions need to begin? Might members start with looking at the membership vows, move on to "How is the church to love the world?" and finish up with "When the congregation says they can't do something they feel God is calling them to do, what are they saying about the presence of the Holy Spirit?" How is God calling you to help your congregation?

[1] From *The United Methodist Hymnal* (Copyright © 1989 by The United Methodist Publishing House); 880, 881, 884, 885.
[2] From *The United Methodist Hymnal*; 34.
[3] From *The New Interpreter's Study Bible* (Abingdon, 2003); 1942, note on John 17:3.

8.

The Glorification of God

John 18:12–19:42; 20–21

Claim Your Story

How do you understand the importance of the crucifixion and resurrection of Jesus? What do you think they communicate about God? Where are the roots of your thinking—who helped you to understand them as you do? Is the most important part of the story simply to believe that the events described really happened? Is the point of the Resurrection for you that God can do the impossible or that it is a faithful thing to believe when it is hard? Or do you find a deeper message at the heart of our faith?

Many people dislike Lent (note the attendance at Lenten and Holy Week services) because it makes them feel guilty. They fear hearing a message that somehow they are responsible for this terrible miscarriage of justice. It's not easy to fill the pews for the purpose of castigating the congregation! Are you among those who have been made to believe that the crucifixion of the Lord is really all about you—how bad you are, how hopeless you are, how pathetic you are? Does Jesus get pretty much left out of the equation? Is God a mere bystander?

A lot of people come at the Resurrection as one more of the "six impossible things to believe before breakfast," assuming that faith means putting aside your critical thinking and just believing what you are told. Is the Resurrection only a celebration of Jesus "beating the rap"? Do you believe that your life with God is really still dependent upon your goodness? Final question: Is your thinking logical? Does it hang together? Does your thinking about the Crucifixion and Resurrection make sense?

Enter the Bible Story

Enthroned on the Cross

Salvador Dali painted one of my favorite pieces of art, *Christ of St. John of the Cross*. ("St. John" does not refer to our Gospel writer.) I was fortunate enough to see the original in a gallery in Glasgow, Scotland. In this painting the crucified Christ is seen from above (God's perspective?). We are looking down at Christ, whose head is bowed so we cannot see his face. Christ is suspended in midair on the cross. The sky behind him is black. Below him, the sun shines behind clouds; and we see fishermen and boats on a lake. But it is in recognizing what is not in the painting that we begin to see a crucified Christ much like the one represented in John's Gospel. There are no nails in Jesus' hands and feet. There is no wound from a sword thrust, no crown of thorns, no blood. Christ is elevated above the earth, above the fishermen.

The emphasis in the painting and in John's Gospel is not on Jesus' suffering or humanity's inhumanity. This is not about historical accuracy. This is Christ enthroned on the cross. This is what is described by Jesus in John's Gospel as being "lifted up" (3:14; 8:28; 12:32). The result of Jesus' crucifixion will be, according to Jesus, "eternal life" for those who believe (3:15) that "I am" and that Jesus does indeed speak what he has heard from God. It is the means by which Christ "will draw everyone" to himself (12:32). The crucifixion of Christ is not some terrible tragedy that God should have put a stop to; it is not for the purpose of showing the cruelty of humankind; and it is not for laying a guilt trip on the faithful. Jesus, in this Gospel, willingly goes to the cross for the purpose of glorifying God—showing God in all God's self-giving love. Christ's obedience even to death in order to glorify God leads to God's glorifying of Christ: "Father, the time has come. Glorify your Son, so that your Son can glorify you" (17:1).

Jesus, in John, is no victim: "No one takes it [my life] from me, but I give it up because I want to" (10:18a). In John's Passion narrative there is no prayer of "let this cup pass"; there is no cry of dereliction from the cross. In John, Jesus is always in control. At Jesus' arrest, Judas never has a chance to identify him. Jesus "went out and asked, 'Who are you looking for?'" (18:4). He then identifies himself. There is no jeering while Jesus is on the cross. There is no final cry but rather the calm words, "It is completed" (19:30). The expressions of Jesus' suffering are almost nonexistent. The center of the story is the action of God through Jesus—the identification of who God is and the glorification of the Father through the action of the Son. It is the truth about the nature of God as pure *agapé*—self-giving love—revealed on the cross, which will draw all humanity to God.

The picture of the disciples in the Passion narrative is instructive. Here are all these people who had walked with Jesus—some for three years—who had seen his signs and who had heard his words. One person betrayed him to his opponents; one denied that he knew him; and the rest (with the exception of his mother and her sister, Mary the wife of Clopas, Mary Magdalene, and the "disciple whom he loved)" ran like scared rabbits (19:25-26).

True Power

The message from God is, in part, that true power is not the power to kill or to destroy. Yet that was the power the disciples trusted as late as the previous evening. Peter had brought a weapon—a sword (18:10). Power was in the hands of the one who could wield violence: the sword of attack, the authority to crucify. How could power be anything else? It looked as though death were in control that Friday—death, the final power. But as the disciples were soon to find out, looks can be deceiving! What looks like weakness turns out to be the power of almighty God. What looks like an unrelieved tragedy turns out to be the victory of God for the whole creation! God seemed to be absent on that dark Friday; but in truth, God was being glorified.

We are not in control of that scene. It's not about us or how bad we are. It's about how good God is. It is Jesus' ultimate revealing of the nature of God: the all-powerful God who is love itself, as the epistle writer says in 1 John 4:8.

Maybe there are things in your life that are really quite different than they appear to be. Maybe that locked door is really an open window. Maybe that failure is the point at which your life will turn in a new direction. Maybe what looks like an ending is really a beginning. The God we have to deal with is, after all, the God who makes the last first and the dead to live. Looks can indeed be deceiving.

Hearing the Complete Gospel Message

I must admit that I get a little tired of hearing the now-trite words of Scripture, "Christ died for our sins" (1 Corinthians 15:3). I didn't say that I don't believe them; I said that I get tired of hearing them. That's because these words are only half the message, and half the message is a distortion of the message. It puts me in mind of my all-time favorite movie, *Crimson Tide*, in which a damaged radio buoy on an American submarine makes it impossible to understand the first part of a message without the second part: Are they to fire on the Soviet Union, or are they not to fire? With only the first half of the message, the gospel word invites guilt: focusing on our sin, our failure. It doesn't define clearly our response and may leave us with the feeling that the Christian's basic stance is sorrow for failure (Now look what you've done!).

We need to hear the Good Friday half of the message along with the Easter message. In theological study, the Crucifixion and Resurrection are usually discussed together: They are two parts of the same event. And the second half of the message that allows the first to make sense is "Christ is risen!" Having given the Son of God over to death, over to what is seen as the absence of God, God now destroys death's perceived power and reputation. God, in the resurrection of Jesus, shows death's power to destroy us to be a phony power. The power of death is a fake and a fraud. It does not have the power to obliterate the love that is the very crux of the nature of God. Death, for all its horrors, is not the final word about humanity.

In John's Gospel, eternal life begins when one sees with the eyes of faith that Jesus is the truth about God, that in Jesus, we are being approached by the God of the universe with an offer of fellowship. Christ died for our sins; but Christ has been raised so that life can begin again, on a new plane. In Chapter 21, the risen Christ asks Peter three times if it is true that Peter loves him. The three denials of Thursday night are thereby acknowledged and then dismissed. What Christ is interested in is not eternal handwringing and slouching guilt. There is work to do; and if Christ's work is to be accomplished, then the church had better get moving. Moping around accomplishes nothing.

This is no advice offered from the sidelines. The command to Peter, and thus to all disciples, is "Follow me" (21:19). Through the Holy Spirit, Christ goes with the church. We are not sent off by ourselves; we go in the power of the Resurrection. John's version of the Pentecost event is found in 20:21-23. The word for "spirit" in Greek is the same as the word for "breath." As the Holy Spirit resided in Jesus during his earthly life, so now the Spirit—the power-filled Spirit of God—resides in the church, giving it everything it needs to accomplish God's will in the world.

Jesus' flock, Jesus tells Peter, needs tending, feeding (21:15-17). Who is this flock? Christ's words take us back to Chapter 10, where Jesus portrays himself as the Good Shepherd, whose sheep know his voice and follow him. The tending of "one another" is uppermost in the teaching of the risen Christ. It is the church that must be carefully tended and nurtured. Note how quickly the thrust of the Resurrection narratives change from the fact of the Resurrection to the importance of the church. But if keeping God's flock is all that is required, why will Peter, and by extension the church, be persecuted (21:18)? Because (dropping the sheep metaphor) the church that is nurtured and tended exists to go into the world as Jesus came into the world and to love the world as God loves the world. This, as we have clearly seen, is a dangerous assignment!

Living the Resurrection Life

Why, then, is the church called by Christ to do these things? One, because in doing them the truth about the love of God is revealed; and two, that is how we participate in real life, resurrection life—the life that is more sure, more powerful, than all the powers of death. Someone has written that the Easter flower should not be the lily, which doesn't bloom

The Witness of Wesley and Others

John Wesley and the faith community that gathered around him tried it in eighteenth-century England and had a very rough go of it. Wesley was attacked and vilified, lost his pulpit, and was hounded by paid hecklers. He had had the audacity to educate and care for the permanent underclass that the factory and mine owners counted on for a cheap supply of labor. By educating children in Sunday school and preaching to them that they were loved by God, Wesley and his kind threatened the status quo and the making of money. For that, the faithful community had to pay.

Closer to our own times, civil rights workers, women's rights advocates, and a host of others in a country that perceives itself as having Christian roots have been called everything from communists to she-devils because, with their love for the oppressed, they have threatened the balance of power—and those in power fight to keep power at all costs.

naturally until the warmth of summer, and then only in well-tended gardens. The true Easter flower should be the dandelion, which blooms early, goes anywhere and everywhere, and seems to be impossible to eradicate! Resurrection life is not hothouse life; it is indestructible life that brings hope and healing to the world. The people of God may be beaten down for a time by the powers that be, but they always come back; and evil finally collapses from Easter's constant assault.

That's why I get tired of the constant refrain "Christ died for our sins" *without* the accompanying statement "Christ is risen! Alleluia!" I sometimes wonder, and maybe it's just me, if the Resurrection gets overshadowed by death and guilt in some churches because it's easier to feel guilty and moan about it than it is to live the resurrection life of following the risen Christ into a suffering world. To be Easter people, the church has to live now and move and make a difference in the world with Christ's love. Sometimes it seems that some sectors of the church have preferred to treat the Resurrection as though it were one more parlor trick that God performed in order to give us one more strange thing to believe. And after we've acknowledged it, it goes back into the attic with the Easter baskets and fake grass.

The Easter message is a frightening, exhilarating, challenging message that calls every Saint Lazarus Church to come forth and live. When a congregation knows itself to be Easter people, those outside the church sit up and take notice. For a congregation that feels the life of Christ coursing through it is going to do the very things out in the world that onlookers have been waiting to see.

Live the Story

What does the Resurrection mean to you? Is it one more of the impossible things you need to believe before breakfast? Or is the Resurrection the offer of living your life on an entirely new plane? Is it the healing of your failures and a call to drop the guilt and follow Christ wherever he leads you? What would it mean for you to live in the Resurrection? How would the world and its powers look different if you could see them through the lens of the Resurrection? How would your life look different seen through the Easter lens?

Easter is like turning to the last page in the book to see how the story turns out. And behold! Life wins! If you know that life is the winner, then the only way to live that makes any sense is to get in line with the life-giving work to which Christ is calling you and his whole church. Volunteers in Haiti; a grief counselor; the activist calling out for justice; the social worker who, in the face of a rotting inner city, cares for her clients day after day: These are Easter people. The question now comes to you: What season is it where you are?

Leader Guide

People often view the Bible as a maze of obscure people, places, and events from centuries ago and struggle to relate it to their daily lives. IMMERSION invites us to experience the Bible as a record of God's loving revelation to humankind. These studies recognize our emotional, spiritual, and intellectual needs and welcome us into the Bible story and into deeper faith.

As leader of an IMMERSION group, you will help participants to encounter the Word of God and the God of the Word that will lead to new creation in Christ. You do not have to be an expert to lead; in fact, you will participate with your group in listening to and applying God's life-transforming Word to your lives. You and your group will explore the building blocks of the Christian faith through key stories, people, ideas, and teachings in every book of the Bible. You will also explore the bridges and points of connection between the Old and New Testaments.

Choosing and Using the Bible

The central goal of IMMERSION is engaging the members of your group with the Bible in a way that informs their minds, forms their hearts, and transforms the way they live out their Christian faith. Participants will need this study book and a Bible. IMMERSION is an excellent accompaniment to the Common English Bible (CEB). It shares with the CEB four common aims: clarity of language, faith in the Bible's power to transform lives, the emotional expectation that people will find the love of God, and the rational expectation that people will find the knowledge of God.

Other recommended study Bibles include *The New Interpreter's Study Bible* (NRSV), *The New Oxford Annotated Study Bible* (NRSV), *The HarperCollins Study Bible* (NRSV); the *NIV and TNIV Study Bibles*, and the *Archaeological Study Bible* (NIV). Encourage participants to use more than one translation. *The Message: The Bible in Contemporary Language* is a modern paraphrase of the Bible, based on the original languages. Eugene H. Peterson has created a masterful presentation of the Scripture text, which is best used alongside rather than in place of the CEB or another primary English translation.

One of the most reliable interpreters of the Bible's meaning is the Bible itself. Invite participants first of all to allow Scripture to have its say. Pay attention to context. Ask questions of the text. Read every passage with curiosity, always seeking to answer the basic Who? What? Where? When? and Why? questions.

Bible study groups should also have handy essential reference resources in case someone wants more information or needs clarification on specific words, terms, concepts, places, or people mentioned in the Bible. A Bible dictionary, Bible atlas, concordance, and one-volume Bible commentary together make for a good, basic reference library.

The Leader's Role

An effective leader prepares ahead. This leader guide provides easy to follow, step-by-step suggestions for leading a group. The key task of the leader is to guide discussion and activities that will engage heart and head and will invite faith development. Discussion questions are included, and you may want to add questions posed by you or your group. Here are suggestions for helping your group engage Scripture:

State questions clearly and simply.

Ask questions that move Bible truths from "outside" (dealing with concepts, ideas, or information about a passage) to "inside" (relating to the experiences, hopes, and dreams of the participants).

Work for variety in your questions, including compare and contrast, information recall, motivation, connections, speculation, and evaluation.

Avoid questions that call for yes-or-no responses or answers that are obvious.

Don't be afraid of silence during a discussion. It often yields especially thoughtful comments.

Test questions before using them by attempting to answer them yourself.

When leading a discussion, pay attention to the mood of your group by "listening" with your eyes as well as your ears.

Guidelines for the Group

IMMERSION is designed to promote full engagement with the Bible for the purpose of growing faith and building up Christian community. While much can be gained from individual reading, a group Bible study offers an ideal setting in which to achieve these aims. Encourage participants to bring their Bibles and read from Scripture during the session. Invite participants to consider the following guidelines as they participate in the group:

Respect differences of interpretation and understanding.

Support one another with Christian kindness, compassion, and courtesy.

Listen to others with the goal of understanding rather than agreeing or disagreeing.

Celebrate the opportunity to grow in faith through Bible study.

Approach the Bible as a dialogue partner, open to the possibility of being challenged or changed by God's Word.

Recognize that each person brings unique and valuable life experiences to the group and is an important part of the community.

Reflect theologically—that is, be attentive to three basic questions: What does this say about God? What does this say about me/us? What does this say about the relationship between God and me/us?

Commit to a *lived faith response* in light of insights you gain from the Bible. In other words, what changes in attitudes (how you believe) or actions (how you behave) are called for by God's Word?

Group Sessions

The group sessions, like the chapters themselves, are built around three sections: "Claim Your Story," "Enter the Bible Story," and "Live the Story." Sessions are designed to move participants from an awareness of their own life story, issues, needs, and experiences into an encounter and dialogue with the story of Scripture and to make decisions integrating their personal stories and the Bible's story.

The session plans in the following pages will provide questions and activities to help your group focus on the particular content of each chapter. In addition to questions and activities, the plans will include chapter title, Scripture, and faith focus.

Here are things to keep in mind for all the sessions:

Prepare Ahead

Study the Scripture, comparing different translations and perhaps a paraphrase.
Read the chapter, and consider what it says about your life and the Scripture.
Gather materials such as large sheets of paper or a markerboard with markers.
Prepare the learning area. Write the faith focus for all to see.

Welcome Participants

Invite participants to greet one another.
Tell them to find one or two people and talk about the faith focus.
Ask: What words stand out for you? Why?

Guide the Session

Look together at "Claim Your Story." Ask participants to give their reactions to the stories and examples given in each chapter. Use questions from the session plan to elicit comments based on personal experiences and insights.

Ask participants to open their Bibles and "Enter the Bible Story." For each portion of Scripture, use questions from the session plan to help participants gain insight into the text and relate it to issues in their own lives.

Step through the activity or questions posed in "Live the Story." Encourage participants to embrace what they have learned and to apply it in their daily lives.

Invite participants to offer their responses or insights about the boxed material in "Across the Testaments," "About the Scripture," and "About the Christian Faith."

Close the Session

Encourage participants to read the following week's Scripture and chapter before the next session.
Offer a closing prayer.

1. The Mystery of God
John 1:1–2:11

Faith Focus

In his nature and ministry, Jesus Christ makes known to us both the transcendent God and the God with us. Like John, we are called to testify to God in Christ.

Before the Session

On a large sheet of paper, print the following: "Who is Jesus? Where did he come from? Where is he going?" Also print the following statement: "The overarching topic of the Gospel of John is the nature and mission of Jesus Christ as the One who makes God known." If you plan to close by reciting the Apostles' Creed, obtain a hymnal with that creed or print it on a large sheet of paper.

Claim Your Story

Invite participants to recall a time when they struggled with feeling lost or without direction, unsure of the next step to take in their lives. What if it is not entirely clear if there is a right direction? How does one shed light on uncertainties in order to clarify a decision? In the Gospel of John, light is one of many metaphors that describe the coming of Jesus into the world.

Enter the Bible Story

Point out the topic of the Gospel, printed on the large sheet of paper. Ask a volunteer to read aloud Psalm 8:1-4, and pose the questions in the study: How can we know such a God? How can we know what God wants of us? Ask the group to read silently Genesis 1:1-4 and then John 1:1-5, noting that both begin with "In the beginning. . ." John speaks about the "Word" being with God and in fact being God. The study tells us that God "pitched [God's] tent" with us by taking human form. What is the difference for us to conceive of a God who dwells with us and lives in the same skin as we do, as opposed to the God who created the vastness of the universe?

John 1:1-18—the Prologue

Call the group's attention to the three questions the study writer says are posed by the Gospel writer. Ask them to name the central themes that the writer states are included in the prologue to the Gospel (the first 18 verses). List these on a separate sheet of paper. Together, define the terms *world* and *eternal life*, and record these on a large sheet of paper. Keep this paper in a safe place. Throughout this study, the group will add to this vocabulary list in order to shed more light on the deep meanings of the writing.

John 1:19-50

The study writer observes that this Gospel underscores a different status for John the Baptizer than in the other Gospels. Note that John defines himself first in terms of who he is not. Here he is the unnamed voice from Isaiah (Isaiah 40:1-3) that calls the people to prepare for the coming of God. Who are the unnamed wilderness voices in our time? How might we prepare ourselves for the presence of God in our lives?

Ask the group to name the metaphors John uses in his testimony about who Jesus is. What is the significance of each metaphor? The study writer observes that it seems strange that people often ascribe to God the Father things they would never in a million years ascribe to Jesus. Ask the group to respond to the writer's assertion that if Jesus reveals God, it is inconsistent to believe, for example, that it is God's will for a young person to die.

Discuss the impulses that led each of the first four disciples to join Jesus. Has anyone in the group experienced someone opening the door to faith for them? Has anyone received an invitation to faith through another, or been drawn to the mystery of Jesus Christ and the power of his message?

John 2:1-11

Rather than miracles, John includes signs that are not proofs of belief, but rather that point to God's presence in Jesus and God's desired relationship with us. What do these signs tell us about the nature of God?

Live the Story

Invite the group to consider in silence these questions from the study: Who is God? How does God want to relate to you? Think of Jesus as the Incarnate Word. Then remember what you can of Jesus' words and actions in all the Gospels. What is God saying to you through Jesus?

The study affirms the Trinity as the three ways God reveals God's self to us: as Father or Creator; as Son, the Word that was incarnate in Jesus; and as the Holy Spirit, God with us enabling us to be the body of Christ. Close by reciting the Apostles' Creed.

2. Jesus Offers Life
John 2:12-22; 3:1-21; 4:4-42; 6:1-59

Faith Focus
Jesus Christ offers us new life, and it is available to everyone. We have only to trust God and to step forward in obedience.

Before the Session
On separate large sheets of paper, print the following: "Is that all there is?" "The one with the most toys when he dies, wins," and "Our hearts are restless till they find rest in Thee." Also try to obtain some white, self-adhesive shelf liner and cut it into strips the size of a bumper sticker, or just cut some white poster board into strips. You'll need permanent, colored, felt-tipped markers and pencils. If you like, check a hymnal for the old hymn "Trust and Obey."

Claim Your Story
Invite participants to read the three statements on the large sheets of paper. Does anyone in the group feel restlessness, emptiness, or a sense of incompleteness in their lives? If participants resonate with feeling a hole in their lives, in what ways do they attempt to fill that hole?

Enter the Bible Story
John 2:12-22
Ask volunteers to read aloud Isaiah 56:6-7 and Revelation 21:22. The study writer uses these passages to delineate the vision of the true Temple and its fulfillment in Jesus Christ, the Lamb. Like the Temple, are there places or situations in the contemporary religious establishment, or even in our own churches, where we see evidence of money grubbing, exclusiveness, or hunger for power? The writer observes that the temple that matters is not a building, but Christ himself. What practices in our congregations indicate we may have forgotten where the source of our power really is?

John 3:1-21
The study writer states that believing a set of things about God is not the same thing as believing in God. What do we believe *about* God? How does believing *in* God make a difference in how we live? What does it mean to participants to be "born from above"? Like others who people John's Gospel, Nicodemus continually misunderstands Jesus because he is thinking literally, not spiritually. What is the difference in these two ways of thinking about being born from above?

In John 3:5 Jesus speaks about the kingdom of God, a rare incidence in John. From last week's large sheet of paper, review the meaning of *eternal life*, John's usual term, and world. Ask participants to check the study for the meaning of the term "believe", and record that on the definition sheet.

Invite the group to recite John 3:16. Given the definitions of the words they just considered, what is John saying about God's love?

John 4:4-42

Ask two participants to take the parts of the woman and Jesus, and to read aloud the dialogue between the two in John 4:7-26. Give these readers a minute or two to read over the text so that they can read just the dialogue, not the narration portion of the text. Ask the rest of the group to listen. Then discuss: At which points is the woman responding to the literal meanings of the words? When is she moving from a sign faith to a living faith? What would happen to our own faith if we could move from our stock arguments about religion to a more authentic faith based in encountering the living Christ in the Word and community?

John 6:1-59

Ask the group what it means to them to do the works of God. What stands in the way of our putting our complete trust in God? When do we look for signs that might serve as "proof" for us? Are there times when we focus on the bread of everyday life—the stuff that consumes our time and attention—to the exclusion of the bread of life?

Live the Story

Invite the group to reflect on the questions posed in the study. Call their attention to the bumper sticker slogan on the large sheet of paper. Distribute the strips, and invite participants to design a bumper sticker that expresses their own sentiments about what life is, when they are really living, or what is most fulfilling. Ask them to share their completed bumper sticker slogans.

Close with a prayer, asking for the Spirit's guidance in opening our lives to true trust and obedience. Or use the hymn "Trust and Obey" as a closing prayer.

3. Do You Want to Live?
John 5:1-18, 19-47, 9:1-12, 13-41

Faith Focus
Jesus reveals his authority and power to act for those who have eyes to see and acknowledge their need to be healed. In doing so, he sheds light on the very nature of God.

Before the Session
Consider how to open these passages for participants without equating darkness or blackness with evil or blindness with ignorance. Reflect on how to explore the metaphors as ways to bring light to the Scriptures while still being sensitive to the different perspectives that persons of color or those living with a disability may bring.

Claim Your Story
Discuss with the group the dilemma that often accompanies a church's desire to grow. Has your congregation experienced persons engaging in behaviors that undermined the overt desire to gain new members? Would you agree that everything changes and that if you're not growing, you're shrinking? What are some key factors that affect church growth?

Ask participants to consider times when they have encountered the opportunity to make a change. Why are people so often afraid to do so?

Enter the Bible Story
John 5:1-18
Ask the group to respond to the study writer's assertion that the man had become content lying by the pool and that he was making excuses for his condition. Do participants agree or disagree with this perspective? Some persons reading this passage reject the assumption that the sick man was somehow responsible for his continuing illness. But are there times, perhaps, when we tolerate bad situations when change *is* possible? How often have we stayed stuck in an untenable situation because we were unwilling to make the changes needed to be freed? Is it sometimes more comfortable to simply make your peace with a job or relationship?

The writer observes that Jesus moves beyond the position of the Jewish authorities (note that "the Jews" is the Gospel writer's shorthand for these authorities), who were intent on keeping the symbols of community at all costs. What are the symbols of religiosity today that we might identify as critical to community? Does the group agree or disagree that such symbols are worthless if they do not center in love of God and neighbor? When have we seen the church substitute rule keeping for love and compassion? Would the group agree or disagree that we can fool ourselves into thinking that keeping a set of rules is a way of engaging God?

John 5:19-47

Recall for the group what the study had to say in the first session about the Trinity—that it represents the three ways God reveals God's self to us: as Father or Creator; as Son, the Word that was incarnate in Jesus; and as the Holy Spirit, God with us enabling us to be the body of Christ. In this passage Jesus delivers a monologue on his relationship with the Father. Ask the group to discuss how they reconcile their understanding of the Trinity with the study writer's assertion here that the Son is subservient to the Father. In the sidebar on page 30, the study writer observes that nowhere in Scripture will you find the statement that Jesus is God. Why not? What does the group make of the writer's argument about the gender of the words here? How is it different to say that Jesus is not God, but rather the physical expression of God's nature?

John 9

The story of the man born blind can be divided into six scenes—verses 1-12, 13-17, 18-23, 24-34, 35-38, and 39-40. Divide the group into six smaller groups or pairs (or if the group is very small, assign a Scripture to individuals) and assign one section to each. Participants should read their passage and then summarize it for the whole group. Discuss the following: What is the progression in the faith of the man born blind? The study writer adheres to the definition of darkness as the absence of light. In this account, what does the Light of the World allow us to see? What is the significance of the Pharisees saying they are disciples of Moses? What are the multiple meanings of blindness revealed in this story?

Live the Story

Invite the group to choose one of the two major narratives considered in this session, and to place themselves in the story. If they choose the story of the man born blind, ask them to enter the story as the man or perhaps as a Pharisee, and to reflect on the questions in the first paragraph under "Live the Story." If they choose the story of the man lying by the pool, ask them to reflect in silence on the questions in the last paragraph under "Live the Story." In what ways does our spiritual blindness or inertia in a particular situation block us from encountering the living God as revealed in Jesus Christ?

4. The Law and Freedom
John 7:1–8:11, 31-38

Faith Focus
When we acknowledge that we serve the God we see in revealed in Jesus, not a list of rules that are impossible to keep, we are free to embrace and celebrate the life God intends us to live.

Before the Session
On a large sheet of paper, print the question "Are you saved?" If possible, download from the Internet the lyrics to Bob Dylan's "Gotta Serve Somebody." If you have a recording of the song, arrange to play it.

Reflect on how you yourself keep sabbath. Do you engage in practices that are renewing, restful, or refreshing? Or is it instead a time to run errands, vacuum the house, or catch up on paperwork at the office? Are Sunday services a time to truly glorify God, or *pro forma* exercises of religiosity?

Claim Your Story
Invite the group to respond, popcorn style, to the question "Are you saved?" Encourage them to make spontaneous responses without over thinking too much. Then ask them to generate a list of do's and don'ts, a checklist of rules to follow that they think might put them on the right side of God. Discuss what makes such a list tempting. Are we able to keep all these rules impeccably? What is the appeal of trying to adhere to certain laws? What is the trap?

Enter the Bible Story
John 7:1-52
Ask a volunteer to read Mark 2:23-27; also ask someone to read Luke 14:1-6. Invite participants to recall their childhood experiences of Sunday. Depending on the ages of participants, they may remember a time when Sunday blue laws were in effect or particular practices were prohibited in their families, such as card playing. Younger persons may have no memory of a time when malls and other stores were closed on Sunday. Ask participants if, in their experience, such laws or family rules were freeing or prohibitive. What does it mean that the sabbath was made for humankind, not humankind for the sabbath? In what ways might we keep sabbath in order that it is built on love and compassion and serves to honor God?

Call the attention of the group to the list of questions you posted in the first session. Point out that the study writer says that "Where is Jesus from?" is one of the core questions of the Gospel. In this passage, the crowds at the Festival of Booths and the Jewish authorities are grappling with the question of Jesus' identity—again taking literally his origins and his authority. Ask: What would you say is the relationship between a person's origins or education or the authority vested in him or her by some power and his or her authentic life as a Christian?

John 8:2-11

Invite group members to close their eyes and listen as you read aloud John 8:2-11, placing themselves in the story. Afterwards, ask the following questions: Who were you in the story? A Pharisee? Someone in the crowd? The adulterous man? The woman caught in adultery? In that role, what were your emotions? Where were you—on the edge of the crowd? Right in the center of things? Perhaps (if the adulterous man) hidden? How do you respond to the way Jesus handles this potentially explosive situation?

The study writer theorizes that when Jesus was writing in the dirt, he was possibly just doodling, gathering his thoughts or keeping his anger in check. Does the group agree this is the most plausible scenario? If not, ask participants to speculate themselves as to what Jesus was writing.

Invite the group to respond to the idea that the way God keeps the law is with compassion and forgiveness and with the offer of a new beginning. How does this understanding of law transform our rule-making, rule-keeping concept? Does such an understanding mean we are free to ignore the kinds of rules that regulate life in a community? How does relationship with others enter in? What does this understanding reveal about the nature of God?

Live the Story

If you have been able to download the lyrics of "Gotta Serve Somebody," or if you have a recording of the song, read the lyrics or play the song. Then invite the group to consider the statement of the song (and of the study) that everyone serves a master. Ask participants to reflect on where they spend their time, energy, and money, and to consider seriously what the things are in their lives that they serve. Are these priorities that free them, or enslave them? Do our lives reveal that we are in right relationship with the living God, or, as in the case of Jesus enemies, is something taking up the space in our lives where Jesus' word should be?

5. Who Is the God Whom Jesus Reveals?
John 6:35; 8:12; 9:5; 10:7, 9, 11, 14; 11:25-6; 14:6; 15:1
John 4:26; 6:20; 8:24, 28, 58; 13:19; 18:5, 6, 8

Faith Focus
In the life and personhood of Jesus we see the incarnate nature of God revealed. In the actions of Jesus we learn what it means to be a disciple: to love one another and to demonstrate love for whomever we encounter.

Before the Session
On separate large sheets of paper, print the chapter titles from J. B. Phillips' book *Your God Is Too Small* listed in the text and display them around your learning space.

Claim Your Story
Point out the posted chapter titles from the book *Your God Is Too Small*. Ask participants to read all the titles, choose one that most closely characterizes an image of God that they hold or may have held in the past, and then go to stand by that title. Ask them to discuss why they chose this image for God with others who also chose it.

Many people invent a god for themselves out of bits and pieces and then may spend their lives trying to appease this self-imagined God. In this session, the group will explore a multifaceted God through the "I am" statements in John's Gospel.

Enter the Bible Story
Old Testament Names for God
Remind participants that the study says that John's Gospel is all about answering three questions, one of which is "Who is Jesus?" This is important because Jesus reveals the nature of God. The "I am" sayings are a specific way the Gospel writer accomplishes this.

The word most often used to describe God in the Old Testament is *hesed*—"loving-kindness" or "steadfast love." Hesed has been described as the kind of love that will not give up, perhaps the sort of love a parent has for a toddler who can be alternately dependent and stubbornly irrational. If this is the most common Old Testament trait used for God, what does this tell us about characterizations of God that focus on vengeance or remoteness?

"I Am" Sayings
Assign to each participant one of the nine "I am" statements that do not include a noun (in a very small group you may need to assign one or more of these verses to a single participant): John 4:26; 6:20; 8:24; 8:28; 8:58; 13:19; 18:5, 18:6, 18:8. Instead of using metaphors for the nature of God, these statements declare that Jesus simply is the incarnation of the nature of God—the God of the Old Testament—Yahweh, the I Am. Ask participants to read the assigned verse and discuss: To whom does Jesus address his

affirmation? What is the response? Is there risk involved in such a bold statement that to see Jesus and what he does is to see the nature of God?

The Seven "I Am's"

Ask the group to name the seven "I am" metaphors where a noun in used, and list these seven on a large sheet of paper with space next to or underneath each metaphor. Define what a metaphor is: a figure of speech in which an expression is used to refer to something that it does not literally denote in order to suggest a similarity. Note that these metaphors point to God the Father, another metaphor. If *Father* is indeed another metaphor for God, as the study writer suggests, what happens when *Father* is the only image a person has for God? Is having just one image the same as making a "graven image" of God? Would J. B. Phillips say that this is an example of making God too small?

In small groups or pairs, have participants choose one of the "I am" sayings, read the passage in which it occurs, and explore what the biblical study has to say about it. To whom is the saying addressed? How does the audience respond? What does this image for God have to say about God's relationship with humankind? Ask each pair or group to report to the total group.

Call the attention to what the study writer says about the nature of God as it has to do with God's relationship to humanity ("God is the source of our real life (bread)" and so forth). List each of these characterizations next to the appropriate "I am" saying.

Live the Story

Invite the group to consider the questions from the study: Is this the God you have in mind when you think of God or when you pray? How much of what you believe about God has its roots in the Scriptures? Where does your God come from? Have you been confronted by the God whom Jesus shows us? How does the God that Jesus shows us affect the way you feel or think or pray or act?

Close with sentence prayers, encouraging participants to begin their prayers with a name for God that evokes something about the nature of God revealed in this session.

6. To Be a Disciple of Jesus Christ
John 12:1-8, 12-19; 13:1-17, 31-35

Faith Focus
To be a disciple of Jesus is to love one another. If we give ourselves to the works of love, we demonstrate that love to the world and thus glorify God.

Before the Session
If you plan to close with a foot or hand washing, obtain several basins and pitchers, as well as soap and towels. If you want to use a scented lotion after the washing, check first to be sure that no one in the group is sensitive to perfumes.

Claim Your Story
Invite the group to consider the two definitions of the word *disciple* in the study and to reflect on whether or not they consider themselves disciples. If so, do they describe themselves as the kind of disciple defined here, or in some other way? If they do not, what is holding them back?

Enter the Bible Story
The last portion of John's Gospel is about discipleship. Just as Jesus' disciples needed to be ready for the time when he was no longer with them, so it is also true that we today need to be ready to be Christ's representatives in the world. To do that, we need to understand more deeply exactly what it means to be a disciple of Christ—and to act on it.

John 12:1-8
Read aloud John 12:1-8. Not only did Mary see who Jesus was when some others did not, she also acted on what she knew, honoring him with an outpouring of extravagant devotion and service. What kinds of acts of service today might represent such an extravagant gesture? What motivated Judas' response? Was it really concern for the poor, or something else?

John 12:12-19
Ask a volunteer to read aloud Zechariah 9:9, the reference cited by the Gospel writer. Note that the study refers to this action of Jesus as a living parable, in which Jesus demonstrates his authority by riding on a donkey as would a king already in command of the city. This action can also be interpreted as one of humility. Jesus' power, the power of self-giving love, brings those who accept him to their knees in thanksgiving and in service. In what ways might we as disciples live out both confidence and humility?

John 13:1-17
Here John focuses on the call to servanthood. Jesus takes the role of a slave in washing his disciples' feet. Remind the group that in the New Testament the phrase *each other*

means "fellow Christians." Christians were to be each other's servants. The world would then look to this fellowship of faith and see there a picture of how life is lived in the kingdom of God. How does the world outside this church view our congregation? Do we serve as a sample of the kingdom that is yet to be? Is it evident that we are a habitation for the Holy Spirit? Do we draw others in because of the example of our common life together? Does the group agree or disagree that when members of a congregation act in unholy ways toward each other, it is a much worse offense than a slight to an individual?

John 13:31-35

Note that the theme of Jesus as the incarnate nature of God is heard in three ways in this biblical text—through the statement about glory; through the reminder that the disciples cannot go where Jesus is going; and in the giving of a commandment, since only God gives commandments.

Point out the information about Maundy Thursday on pages 55–56 and in the sidebar on page 54. The study writer suggests that this instruction to the church is as important as a sacrament, since Christ commanded that Christians must do it and Christ himself participated in it. Ask the group to respond to this question: If loving and serving one another is sacred, what might those outward signs be?

Live the Story

Consider again what discipleship is, and how it is grounded in acts of love and service for one another that demonstrate for the world the nature of this Jesus we follow. Have your ideas about what it means to be a disciple changed? What is still holding you back?

Invite participants to engage in the act of washing each other's feet or hands. Encourage them to reflect on what it means to be a servant in the name of Christ. Close with prayer.

7. The Holy Spirit Creates and Sustains the Church
John 14:15-29; 15:26-27; 16:5-15; 17:1-2

Faith Focus
The Holy Spirit, our constant companion and advocate, empowers us to show the truth of God's love to the world and to love the world, whatever the risk.

Before the Session
On a large sheet of paper, list the following names for the Spirit: Holy Spirit, the Spirit, the Spirit of God, the Spirit of Christ, the Spirit of Jesus, the Advocate, the Helper, the Companion (Paraclete), and the Spirit of Truth. If you plan to close with a hymn, choose one about the Spirit. Obtain paper and pencils or pens.

Claim Your Story
Ask participants to consider the image of the church as a grocery store. If going to church is all about us, what would we want to be on the shelves of that store? Invite them to compose a grocery list of things we might need, expect, or ask for to make ourselves comfortable. What answers the question "What am I going to get out of this?" What "goods and services" do people with this perspective expect? Is this the unconscious expectation of church members we know, or even of ourselves?

Enter the Bible Story
John 14–16: Jesus' Farewell Address
Ask volunteers to read aloud Luke 24:49; Acts 2:1-4; and 1 Corinthians 12:12-13, passages in which the Spirit, named in various ways, is seen as empowering the church. Then ask the group to look at the names for the Spirit listed on the large sheet of paper. Note that various translations of this passage use the terms *Comforter, Counselor,* or *Helper.* The passage looks to a time when Christians would face persecution. Ask participants to consider which of these terms for the Spirit might seem to them the most meaningful if they were being persecuted for their faith. In that context, what would it mean to have the Spirit's presence as comforter, companion, counselor, helper, or advocate?

What are the tasks of the Spirit, according to the study? In what ways might the Spirit's presence be a reminder of the words of Jesus? How might the Spirit make it possible for Christ's followers to testify, and to what extent is the task of testimony made more challenging by persecution? Ask the group to respond to the following questions from the study: In living a life where no one really attacks or challenges what I do, have I succumbed to the ways of the world? Do I get along too well with the world? How can we be comfortable in the world and follow Jesus at the same time?

Ask the group to scan the discussion of the membership vows of The United Methodist Church on pages 62–63. Tell the group you will read aloud each of the two questions of the vows, allowing a time of silence after each. Ask them to reflect on the implications of the vows as to whether or not they can respond with assurance and commitment to what is being asked of them.

Remind the group that the promise of the Holy Spirit's presence came to the faith community, not to any one individual. When the church takes on systems that work against groups of people, has it moved beyond preaching into meddling?

John 17: The High Priestly Prayer

Ask the group to name the three emphases the study writer names in this prayer. Ask them to listen as the prayer is read aloud, and to pray for themselves and the faith community that is the fruition of the word of the disciples.

Invite them to recite John 3:16. Do these words strike us differently if we affirm the assertion that as Jesus was sent into the world to love it, just so was the church? If eternal life is indeed "a life shaped by the knowledge of God as revealed in Jesus," how are we to live out our calling to be church? The study writer states that when the church thinks it lives by the will power of its members, it cuts itself off from the true source. Do you agree or disagree?

Live the Story

The study writer observes that if a congregation has no real theology of ecclesiology, its members will always fail to be what God in Christ created them to be. The study writer also tells us that the Scriptures know nothing of a solitary religion. Ask participants to revisit the "grocery lists" they created at the beginning of the session. After reflecting on the questions posed in the study, invite them to create a list of marching orders that the Spirit might be calling you to follow in order to take your faith community into the world.

If you like, close by singing a hymn about the Spirit.

8. The Glorification of God
John 18:12–19:42; 20–21

Faith Focus
To live as the Easter people is to embrace the life giving work to which Christ calls the whole church. This life, with all its risks, is more powerful than the powers of death.

Before the Session
Display the large sheet of paper from the first session with the questions "Who is Jesus?" "Where did he come from?" "Where is he going?" Locate a copy of the Salvador Dali painting *Christ of St. John of the Cross.* You may locate one in the library in an art reference book. If you have Internet access in your learning space, do a search and refer the group to a website where they can view the painting.

On a large sheet of paper, print the sentences "Christ died for our sins" and "He is risen!" in two columns.

Claim Your Story
Ask the group to try to recall the first time they remember hearing the story of the Crucifixion. What did they understand at that time about the event, or what misunderstandings of terms or events do they remember? How did they feel about it? Frightened? Confused? Consider the questions in the first paragraph of the study, and respond to the following: "I believe the point of the crucifixion and resurrection of Jesus Christ to be . . ."

Enter the Bible Story
Show the group a print of the painting *Christ of St. John of the Cross,* or view it on a website. Invite participants to look closely at the painting, then give their impressions. What is the painter saying about Jesus Christ? The study writer observes that the emphasis in the painting and in John's Gospel is not on Jesus' suffering or on humanity's inhumanity. Rather, here we see Christ enthroned on the cross. How does the group respond to the idea that in John's account, Jesus willingly goes to the cross in order to glorify God? In what way would they say that Christ's obedience leads to God's glorifying him? With which portrayal of the Crucifixion— John's or the ones in the Synoptic Gospels—does the group resonate more? In which accounts would it seem Jesus' divinity is more emphasized? In which is his humanity more emphasized? If you had to choose between Dali's painting or a crucifix as an image that best expressed your view of the Crucifixion, which would you choose?

True Power
The disciples put their trust in the power to kill, despite the fact that their time with Jesus had given them every opportunity to understand the true power of God. When have we trusted in the power of the sword in the face of the Good Fridays of our own lives? Invite the group to consider times when looks have been deceiving in their own lives—when locked doors have been open windows, as the study writer suggests.

The Complete Gospel Message

The study writer observes that she gets a little tired of hearing only "Christ died for our sins," that this is only half the story. Call the attention of the group to the large sheet of paper and ask: What is the trap in only hearing this side of the story? List responses under that sentence. Then ask: What is overlooked if we focus only on "He is risen!"? List those responses.

Invite the group to compare John's version of the Pentecost event in John 20:21-23 with the account in Acts 2. What is common to these accounts? If the power-filled Spirit of God continues to reside in the church today, what is standing in the way of the church doing what it needs to do to accomplish God's will in the world? If indeed the flock that needs to be tended in chapter 22 is the church, to what end? In order to nurture ourselves behind our closed doors, or to accomplish something else? What is—or should be—the risk in going into the world that God loves?

Ask the group to respond to the following: "If the church is the Easter people, we are called to . . ."

Live the Story

Ask the group to imagine viewing the world—and their lives—through the Resurrection lens. What difference does this make in their perspective? The study writer observes that if you know life is the winner, then the only way to live that makes any sense is to live in synch with the life-giving work Christ is calling you to do. Close with prayer, asking the Spirit's guidance in answering to what Christ is calling us to do, as individuals and as a church.

CPSIA information can be obtained
at www.ICGtesting.com
Printed in the USA
LVOW12s0209170616

492881LV00001BC/2/P